A MAP FOR
WILD
HEARTS

ANDREA HANNAH

Printed in the United States of America

First Printing, 2019

ISBN 978-0-578-52172-5

Prismatic Publishing
P.O. Box #642
Novi, MI 48376

www.andreahannah.com

TABLE OF CONTENTS

PART ONE: HOW YOU GOT HERE

PART TWO: HOW TO MAKE A MAP FOR YOUR WILD HEART

PART THREE: TIPS, TRICKS, AND STRATEGIES FOR WHEN YOU START TO FEEL STUCK AGAIN

For my mother and grandmother.
I know you're making cool stuff up there.

INTRODUCTION

Dear Wild Heart,

It isn't a coincidence that I wrote this book while I was totally, completely lost.

The idea for *Wild Hearts* had been marinating in me for almost half my life in various shapes, media, and aliases. There's a coven of beat-up notebooks tucked into bookshelves, boxes, and the basement, each containing seeds of this book. I used to think I was waiting for those notes to tell me what to do with them. Now I realize they were waiting for *me* to be ready.

I had thought I was ready three years ago, shortly after my first book deal. I found myself with more time to dig into this heart-project, but it never happen. I was always too busy, too preoccupied, too unfocused. The truth was that although I found myself in a stable place for the first time in my life, I wasn't yet brave enough. I'd been intimidated by the backbreaking amount of work it would require to connect the dots between my own experiences, the work I've done, and what I know to be true about living a creative life, and *then* translating it into a pragmatic sort of guidebook. *I'll get to it one day*, I told myself. And I saved a draft somewhere in the Cloud.

One day showed up a lot sooner than expected, and with an alarmingly loud knock.

This past year has been among the most challenging of my life, and the most urgent. It's been punctuated with personal turmoil, crippling self-doubt, and a swell of fury over the current state of affairs in the world. I know I'm not alone in that. Just google "depression rates and the United States election" and you'll stumble upon hundreds of charts and data points and analyses about the collective mental health of the country at the moment. Maybe even the world.

But if we're being honest, things haven't felt right for a long time; it's just been easier to ignore until now. There's a white-hot pressure that's been bubbling—relentless competition, crumbling appreciation for art and artists, systemic issues surrounding who gets the opportunity to make art in the first place—that is now reflected back in the mental health of people who desperately just want to make stuff.

We've needed to get ourselves in check for a good, long while.

But you probably already knew that. If you've had a conversation with any type of human being over the past few years, you know. If you've experienced that nagging feeling in your gut or a permanent lump in your throat as the world seems to spin faster and faster and the 24-hour news cycle flicks behind your eyelids while you're trying to dream, you know.

This new phase of the world cannot survive without art. It needs creators to shake off the dust from this explosion and sully their manuscripts with fresh ideas, their hands with acrylics, their fingertips with blisters formed around guitar strings. We need to remember how to create with all that surrounds us—with garden soil and wool and wood—and to tell the stories of our battered, collective heart. We must stay wild-hearted, but also collect data on ourselves and use it for the sake of our own creativity.

This is how I found myself in front of a blinking cursor, writing this particular book at this particular time, even though I was still terrified. Pouring myself into this meant there would be other deadlines I would miss. There would be other projects I'd have to let go of. I'd be required to not only wear my shield, but wield my sword against the depression that pushed in at the edge of my thoughts and naysayers that argued this sort of book isn't needed.

I went through those dusty notebooks and sat on the floor beside my desk, day after day, until something book-shaped began to appear. I worked through my own strategies that formed on the pages, and I clung to them as I untangled my own creative slump. I wrote about my past misdirections, and I wrote from inside this one.

Through all of this, I'm certain more than ever that creativity is essential—to our health, to our humanity, to the world's progress—and now is exactly the time this guidebook had always intended to be written.

Now's the time to unravel our anxieties and create without fear, to pursue what matters to us as if the world depended on it. It just might.

And it all starts with a map.

SPOTTING A CREATIVE
IN THE WILD

Before we get into the thick of it, I want to be clear on what I mean when I use the terms *creative, creative person, artist,* or *maker.* I use these words interchangeably throughout this book, and they all constitute someone who falls under the two categories below:

1. If you have any desire to make anything—literally anything—then you are a creative person.

2. Period.

Mapmaking for your heart isn't just for those blatantly creative people—the visual artists, musicians, novelists. I'll specifically refer to these types of creatives throughout the book to bring home a point or example, but those aren't the only ones who get a say in the creative process.

I'm writing to the guy who meticulously trims his bushes and uproots withering flowers from his garden in order to plant something new. I'm writing to the girl who messes around with sharp-edged tools in her garage. I'm writing to the person who takes extra care to wrap presents with matching, pinstriped ribbons. This guidebook is for anyone who has ever felt the tugging at their chest to *start making something.*

Even when it's inconvenient.

Even when life gets in the way.

Especially when life gets in the way.

THE ART OF GETTING LOST

I also want to be clear that the way in which each person gets lost on their path to higher creativity is individualized according to who *you* are, as a maker and a person.

As I've been talking about this book with friends, relatives, and publishing professionals, I've often been met with a cocked eyebrow or a thin-lipped frown at the mention of the subtitle: *How to Make Art Even When You're Lost*. "Like…mental health stuff?" one friend asked me over a bowl of lo mein. "Where you can't think straight when you're trying to write?"

"Sort of," I told him, ugly-slurping a noodle. "That's how I tend to get myself stuck nowadays. But there are a million different ways to get lost. Probably just as many as there are to make art."

And it's true. Every human on this planet is made up of a sometimes toxic, always beautiful combination of hunger and urge and world-bending experiences. It's pretentious to think we're all going to drift off path in the same way, with the same triggers, for the same amount of time. Your friend in your five o'clock pottery class may be suddenly unable to mold anything other than lumpy ash trays that all look the same, while you may just stop showing up to class all together. Your other friend may come down with an endless smack of sore throats that keep her away from the recording studio, while your cousin seems to be handling things well on the outside…although he's been organizing that spice rack for like a week, but whatever.

Our wants, needs, experiences, and goals all shape the way we respond to the pursuit of creativity. We all may have a little stardust in our veins, but every constellation holds a different shape. For as many ways there are to get off path, there are just as many ways to find your way back.

I realize this seems like a major contradiction—how can I propose a step-by-step guidebook for *all* creatives when there are a million different ways to find your art again?

But this methodology was never meant to be seen as a one-size-fits-all solution. That sort of strict, this-is-the-way" type of advice never holds up well and always dismisses a subset of readers. This book is not that.

Instead, *Wild Hearts* is meant to be a balm to your nerves, a love letter to your creative mind, and an exercise in self-reflection. The point is to let the words settle into your heart and decide what's true *for you*. The goal is to use the checkpoints, quizzes, and prompts as a tool to figure out what, exactly, you need to be successful and how you can make it happen. You may find that on your first read-through, you really vibe with the idea of checklists and routine to get painting on the paper, but the second time, you're attracted to softening into your own personal rhythms. Neither of these approaches are inherently wrong or contradictory. The point is that you get to choose which parts and how much of each idea will help you bloom.

This guidebook is for anyone who feels like they're spinning their wheels on their projects, for anyone who inadvertently replaced pleasure with pressure in their creative practices, for anyone who wants to start taking themselves seriously. Take everything from it that resonates for you, and don't be afraid to leave the rest behind. This is about you, your personalized map, and doing whatever it takes to get your art into the world.

EXAMPLES IN HOW TO GET LOST IN A LIFETIME

The way you've lost yourself now may not always be the way you do it forever. Here are a few of mine:

I.

When I was little, I wanted to be a visual artist for Disney. I'd spend every waking moment slumped over my powder-blue easel, sketching Aladdin or Cinderella or just about every one of the 101 Dalmatians. It was the only thing that made my tense little stomach soften. As the anxiety spread in my veins with age and a rocky, transient home life, my knack for creative detail bled into my surroundings. Instead of splashing paint on canvas, I spent it positioning sleepy-eyed knick knacks on the living room shelves. I obsessed over the angle of the TV remotes, smoothed my bedspread into perfectly straight lines. I arranged my easel at a flawless forty-five degree angle in the corner of my room, and then abandon it for something else that needed to be straightened. Sharp angles and seamless lines became my outlet, and I couldn't figure out how to get my hands messy anymore.

II.

In high school, I learned to run. It started with soccer, where I figured out how to push my body past its limits while still soothing my heartbeat beneath my rib cage. Then came track and field, where I learned that sore muscles and achy joints don't mean you actually have to stop. Pain is just pain, after all, and what does that say about me if something invisible can keep me from flying? So I pushed. I pushed until my bones ached and my tendons screamed and I injured my body to an irreparably dark degree. I ignored my beloved watercolors and notebooks for push-button timers and racing my heartbeat to the finish line. Seconds and milliseconds mattered. Bruises and injuries did not.

III.

That disrespect of my body manifested a different way throughout college. I'd left holes in myself that I couldn't figure out how to patch up again, now that I'd thrown away my paints and given up the idea of painting or drawing for a living. I tried, though, to find a replacement. Overspending at the mall on the weekends and over-drafting the last of my savings was one way to do it, but no amount of polyester ever worked. I craved more. I reached for attention like sunlight stretches for a horizon, attempting to direct someone else's light toward all the empty spaces in me. But holes can't be filled with someone else's almost-love. You've got to stitch them up yourself.

IV.

I tried to fill them in. I started taking my art and writing seriously after my mom died, but I did it in secret when no one was watching. I didn't want anyone to know that I'd stumbling into a new galaxy where words could mean something, and time zig-zagged, and years of chronic stress could start to unravel, especially since I'd taken custody of my little brother. I had *Responsibility* with a capital R now. I let the laundry and the worrying and my family's opinions chip away at my writing time. I hid words like I used to hide vodka bottles in high school—notebooks tucked into bookshelves and laundry baskets, ideas locked out of my mouth so I could never speak them aloud. I smiled a lot instead. I reassured everyone that I was fine, we were fine. Everything was always in order. Our apartment was always clean. My words were always unfinished.

V.

Darkness settled in even as summer bloomed. An impenetrable fog licked at my feet while I typed. I ignored it. It inched further up to my ankles. I half-heartedly kicked it away while I wrote. It crept up further. It reached all the way to my heart before I noticed something wasn't exactly right. I wasn't sad, per se, but I wasn't happy either. My nerves jangled, but the all the extra sleep and chamomile tea never made it go away. My writing slowed. It wasn't until the fog wrapped around my lungs and squeezed so hard that it took my breath away that I realized I needed help. I'd been depressed for a lot longer than I'd realized. It'd been easier to ignore it, push it away, pretend it wasn't infiltrating the spaces between my heart and my words than to admit that I had, once again, ended up lost.

INTERLUDE

THE FOREST

It starts as an interest, a curiosity.

Maybe you don't have to yank yourself out of bed to write today. But just for today. Or maybe your anxiety will lift a little more tomorrow and you'll pick up the guitar again. Or that maybe you need to explore your dad's death in that personal essay you've been meaning to write—just poke around it a little bit to see if you can handle it.

There are a few spindly trees here and there, but you can still see the path. You're fine. This is all good. And so you let yourself wander.

You're in the pit of the forest before you realize that the canopy above you has blotted out the sun. The underbrush whispers beneath your feet, creatures titter in the darkness. You glance down at your boots. The path has slipped out from under you somewhere and the edges of the forest have webbed together. There are trees everywhere, in every direction. The path is gone, and darkness presses in.

It all happened so fast.

It was only supposed to be a curiosity fulfilled, an ill-defined moment.

Every tree looks the same, every landmark hazy. The gray-green of the forest bleeds together in the thrumming of your panicked heart.

Breathe, you tell yourself.

You'll have to start from the beginning. You'll have to go back in time, deconstruct your every move, unstitch every thought pattern until you can identify how you got here.

Where you are.

The only way out is through.

PART ONE

HOW YOU GOT HERE

TRUSTING A
BROKEN COMPASS

ON IDEAS AND THE BIG PICTURE

Never limit yourself because of others' limited imagination.
Never limit others because of your own limited imagination.
— *Mae Jemison*

At age sixteen, Jessica Watson told her parents she was going to circumnavigate the globe. Alone. Never mind that Jessica hadn't sailed solo before, and that her sailing skills were still developing. Or, you know, that she hadn't finished high school yet.

There isn't a record I could find of exactly what her parents told her when she shared her dream with them, but I like to imagine it went something a little like this:

Are you freaking crazy, Jessica? Come on, can't you, like, take a pottery class instead? We'll even pay for it.

Jessica's parents are way more chill than I am, though, and they encouraged her to take the journey. The media weren't so gracious. Several reporters lashed into her after a minor collision during her test run, calling her "irresponsible" and "ignorant to attempt such a feat." * The Australian Childhood Foundation expressed concern that a sixteen-year-old couldn't possibly understand the risks of the trip, and several sailors pushed that she didn't have enough experience to even try it.

The dream's too wild, they told her. *You can't take the ocean.*

You don't have the skills yet.

* Jessica Watson Biography: https://www.wndrwmn.com/jessica-watson

Your boat isn't big enough.

It's too dangerous for someone your age.

It's too dangerous for a girl.

Jessica's dream may have been too big for them, but it was exactly the right size for her. She shot for the long-held record of looping around the Southern Hemisphere as both the youngest woman and at a record-breaking clip, but she didn't quite make the mark on either one. She became the youngest person to make the trek, but she missed a few of her ports on the way due to inclement weather and illness. She didn't break the time record either, but the hull of her ship bumped into Sydney Harbor on May 15th, 2010 to a raucous crowd cheering her on.

When she arrived back on dry land, Jessica insisted that the attempt itself was the dream, explaining, "I wanted to challenge myself and achieve something to be proud of. And yes, I wanted to inspire people. I hated being judged by my appearance and other people's expectations of what a 'little girl' was capable of."

If Jessica would have let the advice of other people and her own fears about her physical limitations get in the way of her biggest dream, she wouldn't have ever made it at all. Period. By flinging herself way out of her comfort zone, she still managed to land within orbit of her goal. She still managed to shatter her own expectations and stay on course.

In any bold new expedition, whether you're an actual explorer like Jessica Watson, or a more metaphorical one like a writer or artist, you'll usually find this question tucked somewhere in the back of your mind:

What if I can't?

There's usually a jolt of excitement, followed by an equal shock of "But maybe that's not for me." You'll come up with this manic plan to write a sweeping fantasy series in verse and sketch out an entire battered notebook full of maps and languages and character ticks, only to drift back down to earth the next morning and trash it all. Or maybe you have the idea to lead your own wilderness retreats and set up writing-camp while you're there, but as you start to do the research of how much time and effort that will take, you throw up your hands and say, "You know what? Maybe I'll have time for this next year."

Or, even worse, you tamp down the whole big, radiant idea. You dim it a little to make it more palatable, for yourself and the people around you who are scrunching up their noses.

Well, I don't need to write this fantasy in verse, really, because it'll be harder to sell that way.

I mean, I could just have a few friends over to write instead of making a website for this wilderness retreat thing.

On and on.

Sometimes we dim the light so much that we snuff it out before we even begin.

This is where we make our biggest mistake. When we squelch what's possible before we even begin, we already cut our opportunity to succeed in half before we've strummed one note or made a single brush stroke.

It needs to be noted here that this is the pit that a lot of women and marginalized creators tend to fall into before they get started. Because here's the thing: society encourages those creators to play it physically safe and quiet their entire lives. It only makes sense that this tendency to downplay ourselves also bleeds into our most outrageous dreams. All creatives have to fight back against this tendency to diminish their ideas, too, but in reality, marginalized creators are up against a systemic bias against the art they want to make. Here is your love note reminding you to not give into the fear of playing safe before you've given yourself the chance to create bigger worlds.

Consider this: if you start with the smallest seed of what's possible, what's left when you don't hit your mark? And we *will* miss our mark. Some of us may overshoot it, or take off a little toward the left, bending the idea in a different direction that we never intended to go. A lot of us will fall short. Our first draft won't be as enigmatic as we'd planned it would. Our guitar skills won't be exactly on par with our dreams. I'm not here to explain why it always seems to happen that way, just that it does. Regular life butts up against creative life, adding an annoying layer to the process of making, and suddenly that portrait you're trying to finish collects dust in the closet.

You may already have a pretty good idea of how this works. A lot of people already do.

A lot of creatives think they have no problem with this area because they can dream up worlds on Jupiter and princesses with poisonous daggers up their sleeves. *How far am I supposed to let myself drift from the shore?* they wonder as they map out a world where earthworms are the ruling species. *I mean, I want some kind of audience.*

But dangers lie in here, too.

Ideas are the most mysterious, subtlest way to drift off path. It happens without us realizing. It happens without our conscious consent. We set our own limits without even knowing, exactly, what our limits are. We just pick and arbitrary point in time, space, and imagination and say that this is it. And, you know, that may work out absolutely fine for us the first time. We may feel comfortable where our creations fall in line within the orbit of our comfort zone.

But then, our beloved grandmother dies.

Our boss or our teacher starts lingering weirdly around us, and we can't shake the sense that she wants to talk to us. And it's not going to be good.

We switch medications.

Our parents divorce.

We get our one hundredth rejection letter on a piece we've been working on for half our lives. It's enough to crack us.

And suddenly, the world seems a lot more claustrophobic.

We shut our windows and close the doors of opportunity on ourselves. *Not now,* we whisper to our most heart-centered, outlandish ideas. *I'm still trying to get my footing.*

Our world—and all potential worlds—get smaller.

This is true not only for our creative life, but in our daily life, too. Our body physically contracts when we're sick. We curl up, tuck our knees to our chest on the coziest piece of furniture we own when we're sick or heartbroken. Our words die in our throat and we stay silent. We move quicker, talk less, and hunch our shoulders up to our ears, hoping no one notices us.

Our imagination does the same thing when we're out of power.

At first, our creative projects may shrink in a variety of ways.

Well, I guess it doesn't have to be earthworms, *exactly. I'll just go back to humans. It's easier.*

You know what? A sweeping, seven-book fantasy series sounds a little too ambitious. I'll write a standalone.

I could throw that Harry Potter themed birthday party, but ugh. Everyone's going to think that's stupid.

Watch your thoughts. Take notice when your projects are slipping back into old tropes that you've already covered, or are easy for you. When you shorten them without their consent. When you dip back into an automatic way of living because it's easier, safer.

This part can be hard to notice. We tell ourselves we're being practical about it. That we're just trying not to waste our own time. But then, slowly, the last bits of our hearts start to bleed out. Our attention turns from the creative work to the regular life realities. We push all of our creative energy into microscopic, unimportant events and it often takes us awhile to notice that we ever made that shift.

I don't really have the brain power to write about princesses today, so I'll just reorganize the pantry for my mom. I could sort all the boxes in ROY-G-BIV order. It'll be fun!

Instead of going into the studio today, why don't I just take the week off? I can get myself organized, clean the house, feel like I've accomplished something so I'm ready to start again next week.

I'm too tired to sew. I'll just work on the holiday cards instead.

We ignore it for too long. We drift from our wild hearts, and we nitpick and micromanage and over-schedule and our thoughts, our ideas, our worlds become small enough for us to stretch out our arms and touch both sides.

And suddenly, we can't remember how we even came up with the idea of space alien earthworms in the first place.

We forgot how to dream up new connections and concoctions and the idea of sailing around a vast, dense ocean feels…mind-boggling. Ignorant. Impossible.

If you feel like you've forgotten how to make something, there is nothing wrong with your imagination.

If you feel like your ideas are dumb and pointless, there is nothing wrong with you.

Your idea, your adventure, is still there, we just have to refocus your vision.

We've gotta draw you a map of oceans and forests and yawning deserts so you can see it *all* and then choose your own path through it.

You'll find exactly where you need to go to make what you want at the end.

USING THE WRONG MAP

ON RELATIONSHIPS AND COMPARISON

If someone isn't what others want them to be, the others become angry.
Everyone seems to have a clear idea of how other people should lead their lives,
but none about his or her own."
— *Paulo Coelho*

Back before YouTube instructions were a thing, my mom used to slip on sheer hose, sensible black pumps, and travel around southeast Michigan, training a group of heavy-lidded Human Resources people on how to use a copy machine. Each day before she left for work, I'd sit at our tiny kitchen table and draw: mermaids, ghosts, horses, in all patterns of spots and sparkles. I'd slip them into her briefcase and click it shut before her blow dryer clicked off, vibrating with silliness at the idea of her snapping open her case to find a love note from me.

One day while she was in the middle of a training, she pulled out my drawing of two snaggletoothed lions. She taught those exhausted, coffee-breathed HR people how to make color copies with *my* artwork, and when she walked through the door later that night, she was beaming. "There's a lady who works in Benefits," she said almost breathlessly, and I couldn't help but wonder what kind of wonderland Benefits must be for her to be this excited. "She has a daughter named Lindsey who's your age and an artist, too! I thought it'd be great if you girls met."

I blinked.

An artist?

She thought I was an artist?

I went to sleep with one of the photocopies of my lopsided lions, examining it, searching for something my mom or that HR lady or whomever ran the world of Benefits may have seen in it, in me. By the time I clicked off my lamp, I'd decided that it was actually, maybe, not that bad. It was kind of good. That maybe I was kind of good, too.

Lindsey, however did not think I was any good.

We met a week later at a musty bar while our moms ordered honey-colored drinks. We ate stale Chex mix from the bar bowls and doodled. Lindsey, a fairy princess. Me, a school of tropical fish.

"What's *that* supposed to be?" Lindsey said, poking her head over my shoulder. She jammed a handful of Chex mix in her mouth and started crunching.

I scrunched up my nose at her. "Uh, fish?" *Duh.*

"Doesn't look like it," she said, licking her fingertips. "Fish don't look like that at all." She picked up her pencil and went back to her fairy wings.

I stared at my paper. It was obviously a fish, right? I mean, the fin did look a little strange but angelfish kind of just *look* like that. I blinked, and suddenly the entire image looked disjointed, like the curve of the lines and carefully shaded shapes didn't belong to each other. It looked like nothing at all.

Lindsey and I continue to meet for mini art sessions every Friday while our moms drank vodka cranberries and dumped quarters in the jukebox (a precious, precious relic of the early 90s). I didn't draw anymore tropical fish. But I did draw fairies. I drew fairies the same shape and color as Lindsey's. I drew their little puffy mushroom houses and their fragile wings, and I did it all while sliding my eyes over Lindsey's freckled shoulder. If she erased a wing, I did too. If Lindsey's hand shook while she placed an open-lipped smile on a fairy, my fairy's lips were just as crooked. And Lindsey noticed.

She sat up to shake out her hands and glanced over at my sheet. "See? Now you're getting the hang of it."

We held up our drawings to show our moms. Lindsey beamed. I stretched my mouth into a smile that looked just like hers but inside I didn't feel much of anything at all.

So what does this encounter with a freckled megalomaniac have to do with getting stuck in your art? Way too much, in my opinion.

I wish I would have had the insight to tell my mom that Lindsey sucked, but I didn't realized she sucked at the time. I hadn't yet realized that art is power, and that sometimes relationships that are supposed to be supportive can end up as destructive. The combination of idealism with a touch of insecurity about your own art, plus too much of the wrong person at the wrong time, can set you on the wrong path. And if you're anything like me, it could take you years to hop back on.

Your creative heart is both a bold pioneer and really freaking scared at the same time. It's *meant* to be filled up with both. You can have the courage to explore new possibilities, to create new worlds from scratch, while also being terrified that you're going to screw it up. The fear part tethers you back to Earth, back to the people you're making for to begin with. What you need to ask yourself is if your tether is a thread or a chain.

Looking over your work with a critical eye with the intention to improve it is a single thread. It's not going to pin you down, but it's enough to keep challenging your own beliefs about yourself and your art.

A chain, on the other hand, is a problem.

The heaviest chains are bound together by knots of insecurity, doubt in our abilities, and resistance to the idea that we may actually be good at this thing we love with all of our fierce, wild hearts. A lot of this false thinking, unfortunately, begins to form when we consistently view our work through the lens of others' unhelpful opinions.

Look, I'm an optimist by nature. I genuinely care about my fellow humans and am actively working to make this world at least a little less crappy. It physically hurts me to say this, but I have to make this clear: *Not everyone is out there protecting your work. Not everyone has your best interest at heart. Sometimes your closest confidantes are the ones holding the chains.*

Starting any new project is generally terrifying. You've fought against your own self-doubt to lift off and you probably have more than enough threads pinning you to planet Earth. I truly believe there isn't an artist out there who isn't initially intimated by the bigness of it all: the idea, the work, the sheer gall you must possess to even try it. If you share this work and your doubts, with someone who is struggling with their own feelings around art, themselves, or their relationships, they may share some "advice" with you that may seem helpful at first glance, but is meant to shut down your work. Even the best of us don't like to be uncomfortable, and the simple act of you pushing your own boundaries is bound to make some of the people around you twitchy.

You can't allow someone else's chains to weigh you down. You cannot carry it for them.

If you've found yourself stuck with a block and can't seem to move into the next phase of your work after such a promising start, check your surroundings. Check your people.

Who have you told and what was their reaction? Did you let someone critique your work too early before you even knew what you were working on just yet? Is your beloved aunt sour on the whole idea of making art for a living, often mumbling something about the "elite artist types who just don't want to work" at Christmas dinner, all while you've been storing that dream in your heart your whole life? Do you have a Lindsey lurking somewhere, constantly telling you that your work is sub par while continuing to work on her own art at the expense of your confidence?

Because making something is usually a solitary experience, we often put the blame on ourselves when something goes awry and we find ourselves in the thick of the forest. We may start to search our pockets for other people's maps. We may squeeze our eyes shut and try to remember what that one artist said about how they make stuff and maybe we should make the same stuff because that seems like a lot better idea since someone's already tested it out for us. It's our fault we didn't think it through. It's our fault we're not good enough. We wind chains around ourselves so tight until we're anchored in the same place, unable to move.

But we must realize that the people in our lives influence our creative work as much as they do our moods and hobbies and holiday parties. It's not our job to carry their insecurities into our work. It's not our job to use the worn-out map they thrust in front of our face. Our job is to listen to the work, without critique at first, and to free ourselves from our own binds.

Lindsey and I stopped drawing together a month later, but by then, the damage had been done. I'd spend the next formative years of my creative life wondering why the fresh hell I couldn't draw sea creatures, and I'd cut loose a few ideas for picture books and paintings involving them. I still, to this day, will tell you I can't draw fish.

I'm still not always sure if that's my voice, or if it's an echo of Lindsey's.

The difference is that I am no longer interested in tethering myself based off of someone else's assumptions of my talent. The difference is that I've learned to make my own map. I check it frequently to see if "listen to toxic person's opinion" is on there anywhere. It's never there. I erased it a long time ago.

So now when that unwanted criticism comes in, we shake off the dirt and the leaves and the stinging feeling under our ribs, and we push on.

FORGETTING TO EXPLORE YOUR SURROUNDINGS

ON PERFECTIONISM

No matter how many hours you spend attempting to render something flawless,
somebody will always be able to find fault with it.
At some point, you really just have to finish your work and release it as is—
if only so that you can go on to make other things with a glad and determined heart.
— Elizabeth Gilbert

I walked away from making art and didn't go back for eight years.

One day I was splashing paint on canvases in my tiny, off-campus apartment, and the next I decided not to pick up the brush. Just for the day. I couldn't get the painting to look exactly like how I wanted it, and I found myself more frustrated than anything whenever I looked at it. I was busy with finals coming up anyway, and I figured that I'd pick it back up in a few days. Those days stretched into weeks. I permanently logged out of my blog, tucked my crochet projects into the closet. As the winter yawned into spring, I'd walk by my canvas in the watery early morning light, alcohol still humming through my veins from the night before, and pretend I didn't see it staring back at me.

The whole episode stretched into a year, and then two. The absence of making things created a vacuum I tried to fill with hazy late-night texts and a breakneck spiral into depression that lasted until I graduated.

I trashed the canvas when I moved out of the apartment. It was unfinished.

The blog got deleted. The yarn got stored in a musty basement.

My mind got really loud.

Everything else became really dark.

There's a false idea about creative types being super chill—at least that's what people who don't actively pursue art tend to think. We're all Type B, they think. We're hippies having a jam sesh with the Universe. We're all about, like, flow, and listening to our hearts and also the direction the wind blows in the trees and definitely not our nagging parents who are screaming *Get a real job!* in the backdrop of our minds.

This, like all stereotypes, A) isn't big enough to hold the entire truth and B) is damaging.

I, for one, do not know what this word "chill" means. I have never been good at "waiting to see what happens", and I can't think of a time where I've ever half-assed anything unless I'm in the middle of a depressive episode. Personally, I subscribe to the Tina Fey School of Productivity. As our founding mother Tina says, and I quote, "Bitches get stuff done."

I like getting stuff done. I get a cheap thrill out of checking an item off a list, and I can say with confidence that I will never be without an analog planner. This is my personal religion.

I do not only finish half the assignment for half the points.

I do not only write a few chapters of a book and scrap it, even if it's in my best interest. (No, I spend a year writing the whole book and *then* scrap it because I'm not gonna quit it, damnit.)

I do not quit on people

I do not do only the bare minimum. With anything.

There's a lot of good in being wired this way, for sure. And now that I've gotten to known myself a little better, I'm all right with it, but there's no denying I have messed up my creative life more times than I can count by striving for perfection.

If you're more of the "I'm just gonna listen to the Universe and see what comes to me" type, then maybe this chapter isn't for you. But if you struggled with anxiety, perfectionism (another form of anxiety), have the tendency to perseverate on the little things when you're overwhelmed, or you just really want to get straight As at The Tina Fey School of Productivity, then we need to have a little talk.

Don't get me wrong, there is merit to putting your entire heart on the line for art that you're determined to make. There's a sacred kind of bravery in that, and you should never regret those moments when you decided to take a leap of faith and do it. Those are the moments that are essential to getting started, and that same grit will help you see it through to the finish.

There are also moments when we tell ourselves how brave and altruistic we are for sticking with a project and we're lying to ourselves.

When we say we are so committed to our art that we have to get it exactly like we've imagined it, we are telling ourselves a story.

When we say we need to take another sketching class or save up money for that big fancy writing conference before we get started on our masterpiece, we are doing a disservice to ourselves.

When we say that we'll get to it when we have more mental energy, time, and space, we are perpetuating a narrative about creativity that insinuates we aren't in charge of our own dreams and desires.

It's time to get real with ourselves and put our "all or nothing" mentality into check.

At least fifty percent of creating something is figuring out how to manage your fear. And by fear I don't necessarily mean the gut-churning, stomach rumbling stuff that crops up before a blind date or a big presentation. I'm talking about all the other ways that fear crops up, too, because fear is kind of an asshole like that.

Fear grows out of the same soil as art, but instead of nourishing your garden, it pulls nutrients from the stuff you need most: the grit, bravery, and determination to get the work done. It can disguise itself as something important, as something that belongs in your garden. It can show up as the voice in your head that tells you *it must be perfect* to be worthy. It can show up as avoidance, procrastination, a sudden obsession with a new hobby, exercise program, or relationship that pulls you away from your art. It can be crippling self-doubt and negative self-talk. It can take the form of anything that gets under your skin.

Like a spindly weed, we need to pull that sucker out. When we do, it'll be messy. We won't get all of the roots the first time; we may never get them all. We will have to keep getting our hands dirty, over and over again, as we dig up all of the tendrils of fear that show up in our garden, and we will continually have to patch up the holes we've left behind. We have to use the bravery that's left behind to take a good look at ways fear cripples our work.

This is part of the creative life. If you're waiting for your garden to be perfect, then you're going to wait a long, long time before something blooms inside you again.

Some ways the Tina Fey type of creative people (which, honestly, I argue is most of us. We all care deeply about our creations so how can we *not* be plagued with self-doubt and the tendency to control the outcome? Anyone?) tend to lose the path are:

- **Sabotaging projects:** Starting a book, and then trashing it after a couple of chapters. Doing it again. And again. Telling ourselves this is normal and we're just looking for "the right" story. Tossing canvases when we mess up on one little corner. Throwing away songs and shoving our guitar into the closet. Telling ourselves that, you know what, maybe producing a podcast isn't actually the thing we want to do. Let's just start over fresh and dump a bunch of money into bullet journaling instead.

- **Sabotaging time.** Telling ourselves that making our art has gotten too stressful so we're just going to take a break until we feel better about it. And then taking a break for the rest of our lives. Stressing about how much time we have to work on something to the point where we don't start at all. Saying "I'll just start again tomorrow." Or Monday. Or the first of the month. And doing it on repeat. Saying that we can only work in the early morning/afternoon/after we have a snack of cheese and crackers, and if we're out of cheese, well then…shrug. Telling ourselves a story about how we think we work—"I can only write in big chunks of time, so now that I have this job, I can't write at all during the week anymore"—without even attempting a messier, but definitely more productive, option. Spending too much time on video games or organizing your dresser drawers when there is a project that's staring at you from the corner of your room.

- **Sabotaging space.** Telling yourself a story about the parameters on your work space even though you're the only one who put them there in the first place—"I can only write on my couch, with my rainbow afghan, with the light of a full moon drifting through an open window." Never allowing yourself the space to make in your own home. Insisting that the weather has to be a certain way, or the temperature at the right degree, to drag out your computer.

Note: There is something to be said about rituals and routines—i.e., that rainbow afghan you always use when you're creating, the peppermint tea you always drink before you draft—to help your brain recognize it's time to shift into creative work. But before we even begin to consider those rituals and routines, we need to break down what you think you already know about yourself. We need to deconstruct your personal myths so that we can build a solid foundation for your creativity, this time based on true self-knowledge.

Half of the process of creation is destruction. It's time for us to light the dynamite.

You don't need the perfect concept.
You don't need to work on the perfect project.
You don't have to have it all figured out before you begin.
You don't have to have the perfect workspace.
You don't have to work at any certain time of day.
You don't have to use the same blanket/font/coffee mug.
You don't have to eat the same snack everyday before you work.
You don't have to.

You are not bound by any time, space, or circumstance. Your work is not bound by any time, space, or circumstance.
You are infinite.

Boom.

IGNORING YOUR NATURAL INSTINCT

ON EMOTIONAL AND MENTAL HEALTH

Learn how to cope, sweet friend. There will always be dark days.
— *Kris Carr*

There are three separate points in my life that I was certain I was going to become a professional tarot reader.

The first was when I was nine, after I'd found my mother's deck in her dresser drawer. I'd made a solid attempt at remembering all the symbols and patterns, but it was a lot more difficult than I'd expected.

The second was when I was nineteen. I'd finally become semi-fluent in reading the cards and had started my own collections of decks in my dorm room. I'd worked up the nerve to read for friends and had grown to like the feeling that hummed through me when I could connect seemingly unrelated dots. But papers and classes pressed in, and the cards began to collect dust in my own dresser drawer.

The third time was a couple of years ago.

I hadn't picked up the cards in months. I had a full-time career, two kids under the age of five, and a house that needed more work done to it than the U.S. government. My brain basically short-circuited out at the end of everyday as I collapsed in bed. Reading the cards was out of the range of possible. That, however, didn't stop me from trying.

I figured I'd start online, considering the rough edges of my life didn't exactly allow for hosting clients in my home and the constant fine layer of sawdust coating my dining room table wasn't what anyone would consider mystical decor. I bought a domain name. Photoshop yawned open on my screen. I invested in the Costco-sized canister of coffee and I got to work on building my new career.

The first week, I started noticed a constant, thumping pain in my forehead. I dismissed it as a stress headache, but no amount of Excedrin gave me any relief. By the second week, I could barely stand being in the same room as my laptop. Every time I couldn't find the font I needed, I raged. Every time I opened up my deck, I groaned. The way the collar of my shirt scratched against my skin engaged me. If my husband lifted an eyebrow at one of my belligerent responses to soapy dishes left to sit in the sink, I swear to you, a demon emerged from somewhere in me and it scared the shit out of everyone. I'd start creating a header, and then delete, delete, delete.

I was hunched over my desk, swearing to myself about font size during the third week when something in me stilled. Time slowed, everything was suddenly crystalline, and I could feel every thump of my heart beneath my rib cage.

I don't actually want to do this.

Something warm pinged in my gut. I knew it was true.

That recognition brought back my previous attempts at this same endeavor. When I was nine and exploring the cards, my irritability had ramped up to the point where I'd thrown my Mom's deck in the trash (and totally went and got it twenty minutes later). When I was nineteen, I became lethargic. Not only did I stop working on my readings, I stopped doing much of anything at all.

This was clearly not the way to go. So why had I been trying it, again and again, for two decades?

The answer flooded me like sunlight skipping across a lake. *This had been a self-directed detour on a path that seemed too difficult to navigate.*

Just before I'd made the decision to start the tarot business, my beloved grandmother had died. Another novel I'd toiled over and tinkered with for years had been rejected. I had been teetering dangerously close to the edge of a depressive episode for longer than I'd wanted to admit.

I had wanted something I could be good at, to strive for, to distract myself with so that I didn't have to bear the pain that had been clawing at the edges of consciousnesses all winter.

It wasn't about reading tarot cards.

It was never about that.

It never is.

I bet if you went up to anyone on the street and asked them to list some words they'd associate with "artist," these are a few they'd come up with:

Emotional.

Erratic.

Over-the-top.

Insane.

Hysterical.

Sensitive.

Hyper-sensitive.

We have something of a reputation, but it's not our fault. History hasn't written creative people kindly, mostly because history was written by those in power, and artists have rarely had access to the sort of power that claimed history in their favor. The only way we write our own truths is within the crevices of our work, and it isn't guaranteed those truths will see the light of day.

That leaves us with little room to explain our weird habits, our penchant for crying in the dark before, during, and after Hallmark holiday movies, or playing the same song on repeat for forty-six hours while we paint a piece based on the metaphors in any Taylor Swift lyrics. Articles and books like this, by the creative, for creatives, are really the only shot we get at explaining how emotions both help and hinder what we're here to do.

So let's get it straight.

Of *course* people who interpret the world and translate it into art are sensitive to their surroundings—both external and within themselves. We are absorbing the thoughts, desires, and emotions of the collective and making other people feel what we feel through a string of words, brush strokes, and music notes. The sensitivity volume's gotta be cranked up for that to happen. And that's not the issue here. The last thing we want to do is unplug the amp.

The issue is because we're so sensitive to the world around us, we often have trouble A) untangling our own feelings from others' and B) reading between the lines on what our feelings actually *mean*. Just like we are able to listen to the world and translate its language for others, emotions, too, are trying to translate our thoughts into information we need to know. Sometimes it's through pure, electric joy. Sometimes it's nonsensical, sweeping sadness over spilt hot cocoa. A lot of time it's Hulk-smashing rage. The key is to figure out which ones actually belong to *you.*

There's a growing body of research about about the effects of other people's emotional states on ours. Researchers have found that both positive and negative emotions tend to spread like a virus—through workplaces, schools, sports teams, and social media.[*]

Basically, your happiness is directly influenced by how happy everyone else in your bubble is. The same goes for crushing sadness, jealousy, and rage. When our grandma is raging over climate change and the heart-crumbling images of starving polar bears in the Arctic, we, too, can feel that same rage. Even if climate change hasn't been a particularly important issue to us in the past. Even if we've never really gotten upset about the news at all.

The fact is that the people around us influence in more ways than we'll ever be able to understand, and it's even easier for sensitive people to pick up emotions that never belonged to us. It's our job to determine what is ours to carry and what we must leave behind. If you've found yourself unexpectedly stuck on a project or piece you originally felt really good about, check who you've been hanging around with. Has your best friend been in a stormy place recently? Have you been pouring your energy into trying to stay positive for her instead of dumping those good vibes into your art? Have your siblings been bickering? Has your cousin been depressed?

Is it possible that you've absorbed their vibes and it's affecting your work?

Is it possible that you've let the way other people feel pull you off course?

On the other hand, let's say you've set yourself up with a pretty stable support system and your relationships are on point. You've picked your project, started the whole thing with gusto, and now…nothing. You're stuck. You barely want to *think* about the thing anymore, let alone open the laptop and pour some words into it. Every time you try to motivate yourself to scribble down lyrics you feel anything but joy: anger, frustration (which is really just anger tied up with a neater bow), overwhelm, exhaustion, despair. One or all of them tend to lurk whenever you get started, and it only seems to be getting worse.

It's time to pay attention. These emotions are messengers, and it's essential that you listen to whatever it is that they're trying to deliver. They are doing the internal translating for you. They know something about your work or yourself that you haven't allowed yourself to think about. They're trying to tell you how you really feel about something you've been ignoring, and they're only going to intensify until you listen up.

A few questions to ask yourself if you've found that you can't seem to get to work lately:

---

[*] Sigal Barsade, 2012. *The Ripple Effect: Emotional Contagion and Its Influence on Group Behavior.* https://repository.upenn.edu/cgi/viewcontent.cgi?article=1101&context=mgmt_papers

- *Have I been nonsensically angry the past few days? Weeks? Months?*
- *Have I been taking out my anger on someone or something else? If so, what or who?*
- *Have I been irritated over seemingly small stuff lately?*
- *Have I been nitpicking, at my artwork, myself, or anything else?*
- *Have my emotions been like a roller coaster recently, where one minute I feel great and the next I'm overwhelmed or upset?*

Note: While I believe that self-examination is critical, I'm not a medical doctor or a therapist. If you ask yourself these questions and realize you've been experiencing pervasive sadness or a pattern of upswing and downswing of emotions for an extended period of time, please go see someone. Please. A major part of creating beautiful things is working toward mental, physical, and emotional health, so we need to do everything it takes to get you there.

Make sure to give yourself time to work through these questions, and when you're ready, tack on a why at the end of each one. *Why have I been furious the past few weeks? Why has the small stuff been gnawing at me?* Press yourself until you get to a broader statement, something you may not have realized was even there:

Because I feel like I have no time to do the work I want to do.

Because I feel like no one respects my art.

These are the messages your emotions are trying to deliver. Pay attention.

When I've sat down and really asked myself these questions, I've been able to slowly loosen the knot that's holding me back. If I can recognize that I've been irrationally annoyed at an internet stranger's posts about his new book, I can start to ask myself why. *Why do I care what he does? Why do I care about his book so much? Why is it bothering me?*

A lot of times the answer looks like this:

Because I wanted to write a book like that someday.

Because I'm mad at myself for not writing it sooner.

Because I'm mad that I didn't give myself permission to try it.

I'm mad that I felt like I needed permission at all.

This process has saved me from a boatload of misdirections. I've figured out that, no, I didn't really want to write the book I thought I did and I've scrapped it. I've discovered that being with certain friends felt more like an obligation than a celebration. I've recognized that I've still been grieving the loss of my beloved grandmother, a year later, and that gaping hole left a mark on my work, too. I realized that maybe starting up a tarot reading business was a move in the wrong direction for me and it wasn't in the cards (pun definitely intended).

Untangling your emotions isn't a perfect process. Getting stuck is anything but swift and neat, and neither will be getting out.

This process reminds me of a video that was circulating around on YouTube for awhile. A full-grown horse was trying to climb its way out of a mud hole. This usually graceful, gorgeous creature digs and claws and makes all sort of feral sounds as it tries to push its way out of there. It knows it's a goner if it stays sunk and it's scrambling for its life. It does not care that some asshole is taping its struggles for his YouTube channel while it grunts and strains and works toward its survival.

That horse is us. Our art is our survival, and the survival of ideas in the world.

We're going to get messy.

It's the only way.

IDENTIFYING YOUR
FAULTY EQUIPMENT

ON STABILITY AND STRUCTURE

She was an adventurer at heart;
but oh how she loved drinking tea from this mug in this chair.
Oh how she loved to be home.
— Unknown

If you were to ask me what I was planning on doing with my life when I was in middle school, I would have told you that I was going to live in a van on the beach and paint streaky watercolors of the sea. Just for a little while. Then I'd make my way to Disney headquarters in my junky ride, drop it off in the parking lot, waltz in and sign a contract to be a storyboard artist for their next animated hit. It seemed like a logical conclusion—I loved Disney movies and I loved to make art. Simple as that.

There was one piece in particular I'd been working on that I was positive would make an impression. It was a watercolor of Ariel from *The Little Mermaid*. I'd been toiling over the exact half-moon curve of her tail, hunted for the most perfect biscuit-colored paint for her skin. It was not remotely perfect, and only moderately good, but it was mine. I'd sprinkled little pieces of myself into it like confetti. I'd managed not to toss the whole thing even when the ocean water bled into the tip of Ariel's tail. In my mind, I was already hauling it into my imaginary shitmobile and heading for the Pacific. In reality, I propped it up against my bedroom wall between a stack of laundry and an old, sagging vanity.

The rain started a few days later.

It pattered on the roof of my mom's car as she drove me to school. It picked up tempo around noon, slapping against my school's windows for hours. While I sat in my sixth hour pottery class trying to mold a lumpy bowl into something respectable, I had one brief, fleeting thought: *I wonder if Mom had someone fix that leak in the roof.*

I got out of the car and sloshed through the puddles that had formed at the bottom of the front steps. I opened the door and trudged to my bedroom. The carpet was bloated at my feet, and it squished when I tiptoed toward the vanity. The whole place smelled like dirty socks and earthworms. Just about every soft surface was soaked, including my painting.

The canvas was streaked with rainwater, reds and green creating a little toxic pool next to the heater. Just like that, Ariel had disappeared into the sea.

Stay with me for a second while I tell you the alternate reality version of what happened next.

In this version, I pick up my ruined canvas, have a big, snot-faced cry about it, and promptly move on with my life. I do that whole "pick yourself up by your bootstraps" thing Boomers seem to fetishize. I make a new painting—this one even more vibrant than the first—and still end up in my shitmobile on Mission Beach. Happily ever after.

This is not what happened.

As fate would have it, that rainstorm didn't just sink my Disney dreams, but it also kickstarted my mom's chronic asthma. Mold spores popped up in the carpet fibers, the waterlogged curtains, the hand towels. This, in combination with years of smoking, resulted in a rapid decline of her health and a touch-and-go hospital stay. Suddenly, I was faced with caring for my younger brother and trying to survive high school without CPS showing up at the door. I gave up the idea of the beach and the watercolors and started applying to local colleges. Serious stuff. Structured stuff. Stuff I wasn't actually made to do.

The truth is, it's freaking *hard* to make art when your roof is caving in, or your mom's in the hospital, or your mind feels like it's full of bees. Think of it this way: If creativity is an act of rebellion against the existing structures in life, how can you create something new when you don't have a working structure to rebel against?

A lot of people seem to think that creatives can live off of sunshine and repressed emotions and still make cool stuff. They forget that we, too, require shelter, water, and food (donuts may or may not be included, but I personally think they belong in the "need" category) to function. We're not going to be able to produce the next Great American

Novel or *any* novel without some sort of security—physical, mental, emotional. It's true that seeds aren't planted so that they can stay curled up in their shell, but they also don't start to unfurl until they know warmth is waiting for them on the other side.

You are not alone in needing some solid ground to stand on in order to put yourself out into the world. Bestselling author Elizabeth Gilbert starts her mornings with a jog, without fail, and then retreats to her office to research and write. One author I know always starts writing sessions with a cup of hot tea and a quiet space. She says it kicks her brain into gear so it can give her body the heads up that it's time to get writing. Another friend of mine—a working artist and novelist—uses a concrete reward system for each phase of his art. Me? I've gotta have a hot drink, warm socks, and the lights dimmed to get any work done around here.

Even the most daring and transient of humans needs some kind of daily structure to keep themselves grounded. Take legendary climber, Conrad Anker. He spends the majority of his time hanging off the side of a mountain, and yet he still builds in some structure to his day. When he's home, he's always up at 5 AM. Anker says, "It's a great time to write or tackle important emails and the like. Before I sit down to think and work, I make a pour-over coffee. It's the first thing I do every day." But incredibly, he also has a routine when he's on a climb. Anker makes sure to thoroughly wash his hands and feet before bed every night to ward off infection and give him a solid ending point to his day.*

If these people need a routine, structure, an anchor point to get their minds ticking, so do you. But it's important to note that no one builds a structure that works for them without first taking a realistic look at their own surroundings, time limits, and weaknesses. You can't figure out where you're going and how you're going to get there until you deal with the gaping holes in your tent or your nonexistent food supply.

That being said, remember this isn't about scheduling a picture-perfect routine. Take inventory of what you have and don't have, jot down some ideas on how to make it better, and move forward with your work.

HOW TO IDENTIFY YOUR FAULTY EQUIPMENT

Take inventory of what you already have.

If you've gotten stuck trying to work on your oil painting or recipe book or screenplay and you can't figure out why, start by making a list of your most basic needs. For

---

* What You Can Learn From The Daily Routines of Top Performers, 2017. https://chasethekangaroo.wordpress.com/2017/02/28/what-you-can-learn-from-the-daily-routines-of-top-performers/

example: Let's say you wanted to work on a cubist portrait of Harry Styles. You'd need a comfortable place to work, snacks, water, a sense of security (like no one is going to bust in the door and laugh at or trash your work), a clear vision, a clear head, a canvas, the right color paints, brushes, a (shirtless?) photograph of Harry, and enough background knowledge on cubism to be able to do the work. Do you have everything you need? Write down anything you think you're lacking.

Get real with how you messed with your own equipment.
Right here is one of the suckiest and most invigorating parts about creating. Whenever you make something from your heart, you're exposing yourself to the world. And not just the good stuff. You're also showing off your personal biases, your misunderstandings and misinterpretations, which is downright scary. Scary enough that we sometimes sabotage our process without even realizing we're the ones who ripped our own holes in our tent.

Take a good look at the list you made. Some items may seem simple, like you don't have the perfect shade of sultry bronze for Harry's hair, or you don't have a large enough canvas to bring out the sharp line of his jaw. But then why haven't you found a way around it yet so that you can make the painting of your dreams?

I want to be clear here that I'm not discounting money. I know it takes funds to buy supplies, and that sometimes you just don't have the funds. If that's the case, I encourage you to take a look at some other options. Could you afford a smaller canvas? Use a different medium? Use your bedroom wall and make it a mural? Sell something out of the garage to come up with the cash?

Even if your list items are more complex, like you're lacking a functional household and your parents won't stop screaming long enough for you to think straight, ask yourself the same questions. Is there somewhere else you could go, like a neighbor's? A friend's? Could you save up some money from your part-time job to buy the world's most effective noise-canceling headphones? Can you work on your painting for that silent hour after work before anyone else gets home?

Here are a few more questions you can ask yourself to get clarity as you work through your list:

- *Do I genuinely feel inspired by this project?*
- *Can I visualize at least a portion of the finished piece?*
- *Do I know what I'm trying to say with this piece?*
- *Do I have the willpower to see this through to the end?*

- *Is this legitimately fun for me?*
- *Do I have the habits or routines in place needed to finish this?*
- *Is it possible that I've been sabotaging myself some how?*
- *Is there some kind of reward I'm getting by* not *working on my art?*
- *In all seriousness, is it more fulfilling to talk about this project than to actually do it?*
- *Is there a way to work around any obstacles I've come across? How?*

I'm going to be honest with you, this exercise is going to piss you right off. If you're anything like me, your first reaction to this prodding is going to be something like, "What the hell? It's not *my* fault that my mom's sick/my roof leaked/I have crippling anxiety." It's going to feel like blame. It's going to make you really, really uncomfortable.

And that's okay.

I promise, it'll be okay.

The reason why I'm asking you to take a deeper look at your own limitations is to show you that you actually don't have any. It's true that some things are very much out of your control, and that is in no way your fault. But. *But.* You don't have to let someone else or somewhere else dictate how you live your creative life. By encouraging you to look for ways you may be blocking yourself from creating, I'm hoping two things happen. 1) You recognize exactly how you got here so you'll know how to get unstuck in the future and 2) You take some of your personal power back into your own hands.

No pressure or anything, but the world really, really needs authentic, innovative artists who use their power to help the rest of us grow. We need you to be able to take inventory of and own your shit before you can become truly limitless in what you can do. Ask yourself the hard questions. Do the work. We need you, desperately.

I'm being straight with you about all this because I needed someone to be straight with me. Sometimes when I'm up late working on a project, that smeared Ariel painting still haunts me. I can't help but wonder what would have happened to her—and to me— if I'd even *tried* to touch her up. If I'd even attempted to figure out how to get a fresh canvas. If someone had been there to tell me to get up, stop crying about what I lost and realize that I'm badass enough to make something even better the second time around.

In the alternate reality version of my story, my fairy godmother carefully opens up my hands and presses a piece of paper into them. She whispers, "This is a little something I came up with to help you start painting again."

I blink. "But I worked so hard on this one."

"So?" She says, "You can work hard on the next one, too."

"I'm heartbroken about it."

"I know, love. I know. But there's a place for that heartbreak in your next work."

I sigh. "Everything in my room is drenched."

"All right, do you want to make it to Disney HQ or not?" She shoos me toward the door. "Better get your bottom to your grandma's basement then. It smells weird, but she's got that old easel down there."

For now, we only have this version of reality. The one where I messed up and gave up and didn't learn to face myself until I was well into adulthood. But eventually, I came around.

In this reality, I get to be your fairy godmother. I'm a little rougher around the edges and I swear a lot more, but I've still got that piece of paper. I gently pressing it into your very capable hands.

This is your map, wild heart.

Let's go on an adventure.

INTERLUDE

THE MAP

Starlight punctures the canopy above you, but you remember now that daylight had warmed your shoulders when you first got here.

And before that, fog pressed against your bedroom windows while you'd packed your supplies: food, a notebook and pencil, and a thick, canvas tent. It isn't much, but you knew from the beginning that you were going to have to take care of yourself on this trip.

In some ways, you have always been prepared to get lost.

If you're going to be a pioneer in this world, some part of you already knew you were destined to veer off course. And so you sit on the damp earth and you slow your heartbeat and you remember. You recollect where you entered the forest, where you wanted to go, and you recall the moment where you pivoted in a different direction.

From the fabric of your thoughts comes a certain kind of clarity, the kind that surfaces with the hard work of brutal self-honesty. You know what happened. You know how you got here.

You pull out that notebook and pencil you somehow knew you'd need, watch the trees shudder under the moonlight, listen for the pulse of the river.

You press your pencil to paper.

And you plan your way out of here.

PART TWO

HOW TO MAKE A MAP
FOR YOUR WILD HEART

THE FOREST AND THE TREE

This section takes an aerial view of the forest *and* examines one single tree at a time to help you map your way to a healthier brain space. Each chapter begins by addressing the creative mindset and process as a whole through anecdotes, examples, and good ol' fashioned storytelling. This is so you can identify your strengths and weaknesses as a creative human being and address who you are and how your thoughts, emotions, memories, and physicality impact your work.

At the end of each chapter, there are two related activities. The first asks you to dig a little deeper into your beliefs and identity as an artist. The second is where we address that one, lonely tree waiting to be noticed: your project.

If you've been struggling with a specific project, or you've been afraid to start, or you aren't sure *where* to start, this is where we take a closer look. Use the *Make Your Map* activities at the end of each chapter to visualize and address that project. These focused activities will flood your work with attention while still giving you the space to do the long-term, expansive work of becoming the healthiest creative you can possibly be. And if you're *really* stuck, feel free to use as many of the *Mapping Modifications* as you see fit. They're there to give you a boost.

As always, take what you need. Leave what you don't.

And listen to the trees.

All of them.

PINPOINT YOUR LOCATION

The vision is true north for the soul.
It is a permanent, intuitive compass direction for a human being.
Every person inevitably strays from the path.
Life is an endless experiment and course correction.
The vision brings one back to the true path.
— Thomas G. Bandy

There was nothing my mom wanted more than a bag of clementines.

She'd called me in the late afternoon as the last threads of sunlight spilled across the snowdrifts outside of my apartment, her tone cheerful at first. "I know you're busy, sweets, but I swear I'm gonna get scurvy if I don't get some Vitamin C around here."

"I know, I know," I'd muttered as I kicked through slush to get to my front door. "I'll get there as soon as I can, okay?"

In truth, I had zero plans to drive through a lingering snowstorm to buy a bag of clementines, and then hand-deliver them to the nursing home where my mother was permanently living. At least not that night. I'd spent the past week strapping all of my possessions into a U-Haul and driving back to frigid Michigan from sweet-breathed Georgia. I'd started a new job that exhausted me. I couldn't even find my winter boots.

There was no other choice, this move home. My mother's prognosis had grown grave while I'd been slumbering to the rhythm of cicadas and ocean tides, and my little brother needed a new home. And still, it left me stiff and hardened, the same way the ice caked around my windows.

I told myself that I had already done enough, that I'd blown up my whole life to be here for her. She didn't need freaking clementines.

She called again at ten, and then again at midnight.

"Mom, I'm not going to the store tonight!" I snapped when I finally picked up.

There was a cough on the other end, then silence. "The fruit isn't great here," she said softly. "I'm really craving some good fruit."

I pinched my eyes shut. "I'll get some tomorrow, okay?"

"Okay," she said, and she dropped off the line with a *click*.

Fast forward six months.

I hovered over a student as she jammed her paintbrush into a puddle of orange. There was a riot of paint on her paper, and neither of us quite knew what she was making, but we didn't care about that. I sank into the plastic chair next to her. "So why orange, Anna?"

Anna shrugged, tugging at the ends of her curly hair. "I guess because it reminds me of my mom."

My stomach knotted as she smoothed out the tiny paint puddles. Orange reminded me of my mom, too.

She'd died a few months before, but I still couldn't erase the color orange from behind my eyelids every time I tried to sleep. The only thing that had soothed me was this work with my students. I'd found the damp flyer for the creative therapy program dangling out of my neighbor's metal mailbox, and I'd called the director an hour later. The whole thing had been a long shot—I don't have a degree in psychology, I'd never attempted any sort of creative therapy with kids—but I'd applied anyway. I was positive that by flooding my free time with more work, more striving, I could dull the clementine-colored ache inside me.

And in some ways, it did.

The pure joy of watching kids paint their fear in lavenders and their hope in blues made everything in me brighten, too. It never totally replaced the orange, but it allowed more hues to exist in my heart.

It was the most technicolored and true I'd ever really felt.

THE NEEDLE MOMENT

At first glance, these two moments in my history seem only loosely tethered together by a color. In reality, they are both ultra specific moments of clarity that contain vital information on which path I needed to follow, a lot like the magnetic needle on a compass. Any moment in your life that's left you with strong emotional resonance when you think about it—no matter how long it's been—is what I like to call a Needle Moment.

Both the memory of my mom and my creative therapy work are sister-moments on the same compass axis. They both tell the story of my heart—my deepest longings and wishes—only one tells it through pain, and the other through joy. When I sit down and really think through them, I've always gone back to this question: *Why does this moment hurt so much? Why does this one feel so good?* For a long time, I'd answer my own question with a tangle of half-truths: *Because I miss my mom. Because I like being around kids. Because I wish I could go back to that time in my life.* And, yeah, there's truth in all of those statements, but it isn't close enough to the core. It's a little like telling someone your location by mentioning you're at a gas station in the middle of a city. What we're looking for is the name of the gas station, the crossroads, and what color cars are parked at the pumps.

There are a lot of moments and memories that make me miss my mom or tap into my enthusiasm for kids, so why do these specific moments matter so much to me? The answer is often a broader, bolder statement. It usually has a lot to do with why you think you're here and the well from which you'll pull a lot of your creative inspiration, whether you realize it or not. For me, the answer sounded like this:

I want to help and connect with people as much as I can, whenever I can, and I love doing that through creative work.

This explains why I felt (and still feel) so much pain surrounding that Needle Moment with my mom and those damn clementines. I love to help. I actively seek situations where I can offer an assist, and I feel fulfilled when I'm able to do so. This was a defining moment in my life where I chose to ignore a request for help from someone I loved most, and it has felt like sandpaper against my heart ever since. This also explains the thrum of joy I felt (and still feel) when I have the capability to help someone through artistic droughts. Some of the best moments of my life have shown up in the form of deep conversations with other creatives, or even unraveling my own self-imposed blocks.

Both your greatest joy *and* greatest sorrow hold the key to your why. These moments are the needle on your compass, and you're not going anywhere until you're positive it's pointing in the direction you need to go.

YOUR WHY AS A CARDINAL DIRECTION

I suspect that if you're reading this book, you've already experienced at least one Needle Moment. A lot of times it's these critical junctions between who we think we are and the direction we want to go that cause us to seek out guidebooks like this in the first place. I know several recent Needle Moments that caused me to write it.

But now that we know what they are, how are we supposed to use them to make art again?

What's this have to do with your map?

Think of it this way: Whenever you're asked to tackle a big project, you have to take the grandest ideas to task first, right? When you sit down to compose an album, you're also noodling through the underlying chords and themes that will weave through the whole thing. When you write a book, you're dreaming up the general plot and the direction you hope the narrative will swing. When you're lost in the woods, you must first figure out which direction you're facing before you can take a single step forward.

That's exactly what we have to do with your own essential memories and emotions before we can draw up a map for your newfound creative process. How can you expect to travel out of the woods when you don't know what will keep you going when things get really, really hard?

There are so many creatives I know that have gotten themselves lost by pursuing projects that never really suited them, or following processes that had been laid out in an authoritative tone on someone else's blog. And they have and will continue to get themselves lost without a clear sense of direction in their creative work, without examining *why* they are attempting to bring these particular pieces into the world. It's really freaking hard to find the path leading you to freedom when you're staring off in the wrong direction, am I right?

The same why that spins through your Needle Moments will also power you through even the darkest parts of the forest. It has the ability to transform the way you think about yourself, your creativity, the way you move through the world. Once you can identify and accept it, your *why* can flood the path with the most brilliant, obvious light. It offers you a balm to cling to when you fall into another hazard on the way to your dreams, and when you are able to chase your dream, you give permission to others around you to do the same. You can literally change the world just by figuring out your own shit. How amazing is that?

When I'm teaching this idea in a workshop, right about now is when someone shouts from the back: "But I just like to write silly, fluffy fan-fiction! I'm not trying to change the world or anything…" This is a solid point, and I can understand where a lot of creatives who label their own work as "fluffy" think that examining pain points and figuring out the broader picture is a bit…*much*. Here's the deal, though: *No matter what you're creating, you're always doing it from within* this *experience, in* this *body you inhabit.* It's impossible to separate yourself and your art from your physical, mental, and emotional experiences, even if you had a childhood straight out of an episode of Mr. Roger's Neighborhood. Who you are impacts what you make, period. Maybe that's the reason you write on the lighter side to begin with. Or maybe you're afraid to face something painful, so you write light. Or maybe you're completely happy writing fluff (which is *great*, by the way. Feel-good art is so critical, especially at this point in history), but figuring out your *why* will help keep you focused through the tough times when you're staring at a blinking cursor.

So let's do the hard work of looking at the joy *and* the pain, okay? Let's allow the wobbliest, most venerable parts of you to build the strongest foundation for your art so that you can stick through it, even when you're thrown off-course. *Especially* when you're thrown off course.

Let's finally allow your heart to point you in the right direction.

CHECKPOINT: DETERMINE YOUR DIRECTION

Directions: Below you'll find a list of the four cardinal directions: North, South, East, and West. Each is followed by 1-3 questions intended to encourage you to dig deeper into your most impactful memories and moments. Give yourself a quiet space to work through these questions. You may not have all of the answers right away. Sometimes the answers will pop up later after you've given yourself a chance to relax. That's totally okay. This whole process isn't always so clear-cut.

NORTH: *Can you name a moment when you felt like something was incredibly, inherently wrong? Where you just knew in your gut that even though everything seemed okay on the surface, everything in you was screaming NO?*

EAST: *Can you recall a moment where you felt incredibly hopeful about the future? Where you felt excited and even a little challenged by the possibility that laid before you? Where you felt like you were ready to meet it with open arms?*

SOUTH: *Is there an experience you can recall where you felt like your body didn't quite belong to you? Where you felt ineffective, or where it couldn't or wouldn't do what you asked of it? What happened and how did you start feeling more confident in your physical body again (if at all)?*

WEST: *What's one memory from your past that you still often think about? What emotions and/or thoughts does this memory bring up? Write out some details surrounding it.*

Pay careful attention to your thought patterns as you work through those cardinal directions. Is there one that you keep going back to, even after you thought you were finished with it? That's usually an indicator that something there needs more exploration.

Also, don't be afraid to riff off this stuff. You may not find every answer you want right away. At first glance, you may see nothing at all that makes you want to create, no pattern that you can recognize. That's okay. Let your mind hopscotch between thoughts and direction points. You may find yourself writing about losing your kitten when you were eight, but that reminds you of your Aunt Penny's vicious cat that you've always loathed, along with Aunt Penny herself. And *that* reminds you of that art teacher you always hated too, and that reminds you of your mistrust of authority figures and anyone telling you what to do.

And *that* can lead you to a deeper understanding of why you want to make the things you do.

This process, this first part of reconciling with yourself, is especially messy. Let it be as messy as it needs to be for you to get there. There's no straight shot out of the forest. The sooner we come to terms with that, the quicker we'll find the break in the trees.

MAKE YOUR MAP: STEP #1

When you have a clear sense of your *why* and can articulate it in 1-2 sentences, head to the blank map paper in the back of this book. In the bottom corner, you'll find a small box with an image of a compass. Write your *why* behind this particular project in the box.

Mapping Modification

If you're having trouble coming up with your why for this project, consider trying this:

- There are three images below. Choose which one you're most attracted to, no explanation needed. Just choose the one that intrigues you the most, or makes you want to take a second look.

- Spend some time with the image. In your mind, describe every part of the image. What do the different elements remind you of? Can you connect any personal experiences to the image? Is there a broader theme there that you're willing to explore?

UNCOVER YOUR LANDMARKS

You do not have to be good.
You do not have to walk on your knees
for a hundred miles through the desert, repenting.
You only have to let the soft animal of your body
love what it loves.
— Mary Oliver

In seventh grade, I wrote an op-ed piece about how raising pigs for slaughter was heartless and inhumane. I'd done my research on the topic—in the form of dusty library books since the Internet wasn't quite a thing yet—and drafted grandiose statements on the immorality of cherishing some animals over others. Not to mention pig-farming is kind of gross.

The day it was due, I floated into the classroom, elated that I'd punctuated my essay with sprawling paragraphs and multisyllabic words. I dropped it onto my English teacher's desk and pretended not to watch as she picked it up and started to read.

My teacher called me over. I hopped out of my chair and tried to keep my face neutral as I approached her desk.

She cleared her throat and said, "Nothing about this essay sounds like you. At all."

She was right, of course. In my best attempt to make my point, I'd copied the tone and style of the articles I'd poured over. As soon as the idea for the essay had bloomed in my mind, I'd started to weave together everything I thought my piece would need to make it shine, and that meant a lot of really big words.

It would take me awhile to appreciate this insight. (Read: I was super pissed.) But this wasn't the first time I'd experienced this particular flavor of feedback. Consider Lindsey story from the first part of this book. I wasted a whole bunch of time trying to draw fairies just as she did. I also ripped off themes and morals from fairytales, the skeletons of characters (if she draws a dagger-wielding dragon master, then I will too!), and the tone and style from my favorite novels.

Even before I could recognize it, my why always told me that connecting with and helping people through creative work is part of who I am, but I had yet to figure out how to generate ideas that were truly *me*. There was a longing inside of me to create for an audience, to say something with my art, to connect. I just hadn't figured out how to be brave enough to let the little things that I loved, things that fascinated and challenged me, find a home in my work.

THE CASE FOR NATURAL NAVIGATION

Before Siri was around to tell us to take a right, people still managed to find their way around the globe. They loaded up supplies in canoes and catamarans, rafted down rivers, and clawed their way through the world's most unforgiving terrain by foot. Their compasses pointed them in the right direction, but it was the connections between the stars and earth that finally led them home.

The boldest explorers understood if they were going to get to their destination, the compass alone wouldn't cut it. On top of this essential tool, they observed every inch of their surroundings: the pattern the stars made above them, the shape of the woodlands around them, the sound of the ocean crashing beside them. They actively observed the unique bits and pieces of their environment and then marked those oddities in their minds and on their maps. They analyzed where they were, now, so that they could continue to push forward without fear of losing their way.

Creating art isn't so different.

Even if we're traveling in the right direction, our work can only carry the amount of impact that we allow within ourselves. By including *all* parts of who we are, we bring a unique sense of authenticity to our art and give ourselves permission to be seen. We generate ideas that mean something, and that are actually pleasant to pursue.

We observe connections within our internal landscape, thus making connections to our audience.

The path becomes clearer.

IDENTIFYING LANDMARKS OF WHAT YOU LOVE

Within each of us, there are physical, emotional, and mental landmarks we tend to return to in our work, or are attracted to in others' work. When we encounter them, we almost always notice—whether we feel a flip-flop in our stomach, our pulse rockets, or curiosity pulls at us. These landmarks could be as small and seemingly insignificant as a weather pattern we prefer, or as heavy as a pervasive mood we like our books and movies to encompass. Below you'll find specifics on each of these patterns.

Physical Landmarks:

These are the landmarks that light up your senses whenever you encounter them. These can be anything from a specific shade of blue, to the acrid scent of the paper mill down the street from your old home, to the way your grandmother's papery skin felt against yours. An example of some physical landmarks that show up again and again for me are: snowdrifts, the scent of earthworms in the spring, sandalwood perfume, the color of clementines, and the taste of English breakfast tea with honey.

Emotional Landmarks:

These landmarks take a little more digging to uncover, as they're all internal reactions to the world around you. Most often they appear as moods and themes that you tend to veer toward when you choose books, movies, and television shows to consume. Many times these landmarks also have roots in our past experiences, both positive and negative. A few examples of emotional landmarks that I keep coming back to in my work are: that pervasive, all-encompassing sense of longing for someone or something, the shame of secrets, and the blind stubbornness of what it means to be hopeful.

Mental Landmarks:

Whereas physical and emotional landscapes often arise from associations with our past or hopes for our future, mental landmarks almost always show up in the form of blatant curiosity. They're often questions that nag at us, bits and pieces we'd love to find the answer to. They can also show up in the media choices we make. Some examples of mental landmarks I'm always eager to explore are: *Who would I be if my mom hadn't died when I was so young? What makes a person pivot toward darkness? What would it be like to lose someone and never find them again?* Most of my favorite books linger around these questions, including the ones I write.

CONNECTING YOUR WHY TO YOUR LANDMARKS

I'll be the first to tell you there's no perfect equation for a nonlinear process like creativity. Our minds, bodies, experiences, preferences, and processes are all too divergent to make the assumption that there is *one* answer for generating an idea that you'll be able to stick with when everything around you really, really sucks. That being said, I've often found a solid starting point to my project when I use the following formula:

Your Why + (Mental Landmark + Emotional Landmark) + (Physical Landmark x 3)

Let's break it down.

First things first, it's always a good idea to have your why front and center when you're dreaming up a project, as this is your compass point that will continue to push you past the tedious revisions and terrible reviews and overall shitty days. For the purpose of this example, let's say you've figured out your why is this: *I want to explore what it means to survive a childhood trauma and work to move past it.*

On top of that that, it helps to choose *one* overarching question that you are just itching to explore more, and then inject it with an emotion or theme you tend to trend toward. These two might naturally go hand-in-hand, or they may seem totally unrelated. For example, let's say you want to explore the idea of how a person finds strength in adversity, but the "mood" you're attracted to is more of a bright, happy-go-lucky vibe. *This is okay.* Keep them both in your formula. You'd be surprised what original ideas show up when you combine two totally unrelated elements.

After you have that down, it's time to dream up three physical landmarks that you'd love to place somewhere in your work. Again, these can be unrelated. An example might be: sweeping, golden plains, frogs, and the taste of cinnamon.

When you snap all of these pieces into place, your initial idea might look a little something like this:

I'm going to write a novel about a young girl who survived a tornado that destroyed her entire town and killed her parents. It's going to take place in Kansas, she'll have an obsession with frogs because she dreams of what it would be like to live near water and out of Tornado Alley, and the girl she falls in love with smells like cinnamon. It'll have a lighter vibe as she figures out how to push past what happened to her and start a new life.

Not bad, right?

You may feel a jolt of excitement when you first do this, and recognize an idea that you want to pursue right away. Or, whatever you generate here may end up being a springboard for another idea. You may take pieces of this idea, add in others, and tweak it all until it feels right. You'll know you've got something that you can stick with for the long haul when you're excited and eager to get started.

NAVIGATING MY OWN WORK: AN EXAMPLE

As poet and naturalist Mary Oliver writes in her poem, *Wild Geese,* "You only have to let the soft animal of your body love what it loves." Once I accepted that I loved what I love, without condition or expectation, I began to let my curiosities and interests marinate in my stories, and they became much better for it. Using this formula, I dreamt up the idea for my first book, *Of Scars and Stardust.* I connected my urge to connect with and help people through creative work with the exploration of this question: *How can someone possibly survive losing the person they love most without losing a piece of themselves?* The tone of the book was melancholic as my main character, Claire, searched endlessly through her hometown and her own memories for her missing sister. Some physical landmarks I chose for this book were: crumpled cornfields in the winter, knitted birds, and cherry-flavored lip balm.

This was the first project I saw through to the end after years of rejection on my previous novel. And even though *Scars* is considered off-the-cuff and a bit strange, I wouldn't change any of those initial creative decisions for anything. It was the first thing I'd written that was truly *me.*

CHECKPOINT: MAP YOUR LANDMARKS

Directions: Using the boxes below, jot down as many physical, emotional, and mental landmarks you can dream up. *Remember, there are no wrong answers here.* Let yourself love what you love! It's helpful to come up with more than three for each one, as you may want to tweak your formula and add in something else later. And don't give yourself a timeline for this. You may be able to finish it in one sitting, or you may think you're done only to come back to it later.

When you feel like you're finished, you'll choose a forest-related symbol to represent each type of landmark. On my own personal map, I've chosen a pine tree to represent each of my physical landmarks, a boulder for my emotional ones, and a squirrel for my mental ones (because those questions always seem to chatter in my ear, and because squirrels are just cute).

PHYSICAL LANDMARK SYMBOL:	IDEAS:
EMOTIONAL LANDMARK SYMBOL:	IDEAS:
MENTAL LANDMARK SYMBOL:	IDEAS:

MAKE YOUR MAP: STEP #2

After you have your symbol and ideas down, go back to your map paper in the back of this book to draw up your forest. Draw a symbol anywhere you want to represent each idea, and write down the idea beneath it. You'll reference this map and these landmarks, again and again, as you work through this project.

Mapping Modification

Instead of spending time thinking up your symbols, let's make it a bit easier. Here's a list of symbols you can insert in your forest that will represent each of the following landmarks:

- **Boulder:** *A physical barrier/injury*
- **Clearing:** *A physical accomplishment (running a race, getting healthy, etc.)*
- **Pond:** *An emotionally difficult experience*
- **Squirrel:** *A joyful memory*
- **Pine tree:** *A question/theme that haunts you*
- **Birch tree:** *A question/idea that you're itching to explore*

RECALCULATE YOUR
TRUE NORTH

If I didn't define myself for myself,
I would be crunched into other people's fantasies for me and eaten alive.
— *Audre Lorde*

I wrote my first book in kindergarten. It was a crayon-laden masterpiece about mice bludgeoning an autocratic cat with a baseball bat and escaping to freedom. It's amazing to me now the people around me didn't yet recognize that 1) I had the sort of imagination that needed to be put to use regularly and 2) weren't afraid I might actually kill someone.

Rather than seeing a talent for super weird storytelling, my teacher urged me to "put that imagination to good use on more realistic stories." She encouraged me to write about people, not animals. To tick off things I'd done during winter break—*fun, innocuous* things—not taking someone out with a baseball bat. (You're welcome, Beyoncé. You can have that one.)

And thus, a budding essayist was born, before I even knew what an essay was.

I spent the next few years writing exposition about my mother's messy kitchen and the way my dad scrubbed his knickknacks clean until his cloths wore thin in the middle. I wrote about snow flurries on windowpanes, the scent of strawberry pie, and that scathing op-ed on pig farming.

Stacks of composition notebooks lived permanently on my desk, a monochromatic snapshot of my thoughts. The easel my mom had bought me for my eighth birthday still sat in the corner, collecting dust.

"What do you think about maybe taking an art class?" my mom asked one day, sinking into the edge of my bed.

I shrugged. "I don't know."

She set her hand on top of mine. "I've seen you draw, sweets. You've got a lot of natural talent. Why don't you try it? You could even be an artist one day!"

I paused. Visions of me standing at that blanched easel, painting a rainbow into reality bloomed behind my eyelids. *It would be kind of nice to do something else,* I thought. *Something with a little more color.*

My mom was a rainbow of a human with a knack for creating. It couldn't hurt to absorb a little more of that sort of thing, could it?

And so, I became an artist.

The notebooks found a new home in the back of my closet while I painted the Disney characters my mom adored. I painted drippy replicas of the daisies she loved, big, dopey sheepdogs she always dreamed she could own, and only occasionally my mind would drift back to my notebooks.

During my junior year of high school, my dad sat me down. "Have you thought about what you want to do for college?" he'd asked, rubbing his thumb back and forth over his knuckles.

"Art?" I said, wincing. It was almost the same thing as a swear to someone as logical and left-brained as my dad.

He rubbed his knuckles until the skin turned raw and pink.

"Art...history?"

He sighed.

I chewed my lip, thinking. "Art...teacher?"

"Teacher? I didn't realize you had any interest in that." He dropped his hands into his lap and smiled.

I smiled, too. "Yeah, I mean, maybe."

"They have good benefits, you know," he continued. "Steady pay, a pension. If you go into something more practical, like English, it could be a really stable sort of job to get yourself into."

"Oh. Yeah, that's what I was thinking, too," I said, even though I had no idea what a pension was or why it should matter. "I'll look into it."

And thus, a teacher was born.

I took creative writing classes on the side, injected my education degree with a major in English literature. I taught those art therapy classes to kids in the community while continuing on with my late-night love affair with drawing. And then, like ivy spreading across a window, my itch to write choked out everything else.

I wrote on my lunch break. I wrote in my car. I wrote in my head and on limp napkins and sticky notes the color of Easter eggs. I found some of my old composition notebooks, and I wrote in the margins of those, too.

I came back around.

I became, of all things, a writer.

THE DANGER OF OUTSIDE VOICES

Sometimes I wonder what my path would have looked like if I'd tuned out all those opinions over the years. I suspect that I would have come back to writing much sooner, if I'd ever left it at all. I also still wonder if this is why I still tell myself the story that I can't write fantasy very well, that I should stick to more realistic writing. My anthropomorphic mice wielding baseball bats have stayed quiet in my mind.

There's definitely something to be said for listening to the voices around you, especially the people who love you and genuinely have your best interest at heart. Every creative needs a support system and a series of voices to help soothe and guide them through this work, but it's essential that we establish our own true voice before we do so. Without getting to know our own voice on an intimate level, it becomes impossible to distinguish how *we* really want to bring our art into the world versus how *others* would like us to do it. And the thing about listening to other voices is that we never really know if what they're saying is in our best interest. Only we can do that for ourselves.

DISTINGUISHING OTHER VOICES FROM YOUR OWN

At this point in the mapmaking process, you may feel ready to get started on a specific project. You may have already started jotting down some ideas, outlining, or organizing paint swatches. Or you may not have felt inspired to do any of those things yet, and that's okay, too. What matters most is you take the time to figure out what *your* voice sounds like and what it's trying to tell you before you dive all the way in. Because here's the thing: There's your voice gently guiding you toward decision that will light up your art and your heart, and there's literally...everything else. Even the voices we *think* are ours are just disguised as more critical, unforgiving versions of our insecurities. Those voices don't get a say in what we're making, period.

Here are a few ways to identify voices that don't belong to you:

- **You start to insert someone else's work into your own.** It's inevitable that you're going to pull from other art as you make your own, because that's the way it works. All creativity is inspired by other acts of creativity, and nothing exists in a vacuum. But if you find yourself adding in elements of someone else's work— like making your manuscript into an epic fantasy when you were aiming for a thriller, especially if you've recently read some kind of fantasy—take note. You may be absorbing someone else's voice and style instead of cultivating your own.

- **You start hearing your mom/dad/pastor/toxic friend's voice in your head as you work.** You may discover as you're starting to write down some ideas, you find yourself muttering words and phrases that you've heard somewhere before, but that you've never used with any regularity. For example, I always hear the word "practical" whenever I start to outline a new book. *Come on, Andrea, just be a little more practical about it.* This is a word that has never belonged to me, but it has flavored every important conversation I've ever had with my dad. Listen closely for the words and phrases you tell yourself as you start bringing this project into reality, especially the ones that are extremely critical. My bet is that they aren't actually your words at all.

- **You second guess your compass point and landmarks.** If you felt pretty good when you figured out your why and identified some meaningful landmarks, but now find it's all not really vibing, pay close attention. It's possible that you've veered off course, but a lot of the time you'll find another voice telling you that this is too hard, that you aren't good enough, that your art doesn't really matter anyway. This is the voice of your inner critic, the fear that we all have lodged within us. That fear's purpose is to keep us safe, and while I can't blame it for trying to do its job, it's still just another voice that isn't who *you* are and what you represent.

At the end of this exploration, you should have a pretty good handle on which voices have infiltrated your creative process, including those of other artists you admire, critical people in your life, and your own fear.

But what's left?

Even if you can identify what *isn't* yours, it can still be difficult to get a handle on which thoughts and ideas are truly yours. In the next activity, we're going to take a shortcut through your mind's subliminal messaging to uncover what your inner voice is actually saying about yourself and your art. Once you're clear on what your voice is trying to tell you, you'll be able to piece together your project with an unyielding clarity, even when those other nit-picky voices inevitably try to cram their way back in.

CHECKPOINT: RESETTING YOUR TRUE NORTH

Directions: Carefully read through the paragraphs below. Each time you encounter a blank space, fill in the *first word* that comes to mind and fits the appropriate description without overthinking it. *The not overthinking it part is key.* Oftentimes your voice tries to speak quickly before its drowned out by all of the louder, more persistent voices, so let's give it a chance to say what it needs to say this time, okay?

You're standing in the middle of a dense woodlands. As far as you can see, there's no path forward, no path behind you, and any way out has dissolved with weather and time.

Then you notice the glint of light.

You push through a knot of trees and kick through the underbrush to find a full-length mirror framed in gold. Tentatively, you stand in front of it and see yourself, wild-eyed and disheveled.

You reach forward to touch the glass, but as you do, your reflection transforms. Suddenly, your face is brighter, your hair smoothed back. Your reflection smiles gently at you as it reaches through the mirror and hands you _____ (noun). You take the gift, surprised, and hold it in your palms. It feels _____ (texture or weight), and when you think about it, it almost reminds you of _____ (feeling or emotion).

"That's to keep you wild," your reflection says. You place it in your bag.

"This one's to keep you true," your reflection tells you. "Keep it with you at all times. It will protect you when you need it most." You reach out your hands, and surprisingly, your reflection hands you one more gift, a _____ (noun). It doesn't make sense at first, but then you notice the inscription along the side. The three words read: _____ _____ _____ (three words).

You pack both gifts in your bag. As you do, your reflection disappears. In its place is the image of a clear, dirt path woven between the trees. You sling your pack over your shoulder, step into the mirror, and make your way home.

When you've filled in all the blanks, take a few minutes to re-read what you came up with. Reflect on the gifts that your mirror-image gave you and how those items could represent your inner resources, no matter how strange they may seem. How could the first item represent the bravery you need to keep going? How could the second serve as a reminder to help you stay the course?

Every time I've done this Mad Lib, my answers initially make zero sense. Most recently when I did this, the first item I received was a crusty, old birdhouse that felt like past memories. The second was a sprig of fresh lavender with the inscription *you are safe* on the stem. At the time I was just starting to crack open a new project that pushed me well out of my comfort zone, and I'd been dealing with a series of false starts. The birdhouse reminded me I needed to be brave enough to leave crusty, irrelevant memories behind to do this work, and the lavender (a scent I associate with calm), reminded me that it's safe for me to explore my creativity in this way, even if I haven't always felt that in the past.

My true, inner voice was trying to deliver this message: *My memories don't own my work, and it's safe for me to outgrow them.*

I'm grateful I got that message, because as it turned out, I received a lot of pushback on this particular project from the people around me. I began to doubt myself, and my fear-voice started to creep back in. *What if you were wrong?* it whispered.

I wasn't wrong. I put my nose to the grindstone and stuck with this project, constantly reminding myself that it was safe to do this work. And I've never regretted it since. The process made me a stronger writer and a braver human being.

What message is your voice trying to tell you?

Again, don't overthink this. Don't stare at your answers and try to smash them together into a pattern that makes sense to you. Let yourself relax into the idea that you aren't quite sure just yet, and make your best guess at what you think the message may be. It'll come to you when you need it, and when it does, it will make you feel empowered, hopeful, and deeply understood.

Trust in that voice.

Trust in yourself.

MAKE YOUR MAP: STEP #3

Go back to your map and draw a path through your trees and other landmarks. This path can look anyway you want, be any length you want it to be, and end wherever you see fit. Along the path, write down the messages you've received from your inner voice, of if you'd prefer, write it on a sticky note and attach it to the map, your mirror, or anywhere else where you'll be able to look at it often.

Mapping Modification

If you're struggling to come up with your message, it's completely okay to just draw in the path for now. This process—and this chapter in particular—is all about trusting yourself, so go ahead and draw in that path with the intention that the message will show up when it's ready. In the meantime, allow yourself to be open to anything that comes through, even if it doesn't sound the way you expected. *Especially* if it doesn't sound the way you expected.

BUILD YOUR FIRE

Just because you are soft doesn't mean you are not a force.
Honey and wildfire are both the color gold.
— Victoria Erickson

I booked a plane ticket to Africa a few months after my mom died. Never mind that I was completely broke and had just taken over legal guardianship of my thirteen-year-old brother, or that we were already a couple months behind on rent. All I knew was it felt like I would literally die if I didn't separate my physical body from this new shape my life had taken without my consent. *I'll get some clarity there,* I told myself as I shoved another t-shirt in my backpack. I'd spit all the fear and grief out into a travel journal and I'd come back a better person. Maybe even the kind of person who didn't run when things got hard.

Instead I spent the better part of a month fumbling aimlessly through Rwanda and Kenya, picking fights with family members thousands of miles away while I holed up in Internet cafes. My thoughts swarmed dangerously close to self-harm, and I found myself looking over stucco rooftops in Kigali, wondering if it would matter if I even went back. Eventually, I ran out of money and had no choice but to board a flight back to the Midwest.

When I got home, my life still held the same shape, but it was a little more fragile now. I'd chipped the edges of my most loyal relationships by running, which only made facing this new, crushing responsibility pretty much unbearable.

As I unpacked my bag, I found my travel journal smashed at the bottom. It was still empty.

THE INTERNAL WILDFIRE:
ON DESTRUCTIVE THOUGHTS AND EMOTIONS

Even before my mom died, I'd been taking medication to treat anxiety and had been in therapy for a short period of time. All of that discontinued as I graduated college, switched jobs, and moved back home to take care of my brother. My own mind became such a painful place to exist that had made a habit out of slamming the escape button on everything. *Work too much to deal with? Delete the emails. Argument with my BFF? Cancel her.* By the time I booked that flight to Africa, I was desperate enough to get away from myself that I was willing to take an eighteen hour flight to get there.

I didn't find what I wanted. Despite being surrounded by the lush mountains of Rwanda and the silty, brick-colored plains of Kenya, I was miserable. My mind wouldn't allow me to absorb the peace I'd so desperately craved, and no matter how hard I tried, I'd find myself sweating in another Internet cafe, typing out *another* tirade in an attempt to gain some sort of control over the situation. And even though I gave it my best effort, I still ended up back at home, even more depressed than I left, and facing the inevitable: myself.

I won't sit here and pretend to know the ins and outs of mental and emotional health, but I do know a little bit about my own anxiety and depression. I know that the toxic combination of them both left me with a wildfire of harmful thoughts and incontrollable fury, and I didn't see it lingering around the edges at first. *I'm fine*, I'd tell myself as I jabbed out another tyrannical email, *I'm just telling them what needs to be said.*

What actually needed to be said was that everything was burning.

If attention is power, then avoidance is the rejection of self-knowledge. I had avoided the scent of smoke and the bleating of alarms for so long that everything had to be destroyed for me to pay attention. By the time I walked back through my front door, the pain was more persistent than when I'd left.

Because here is a cringeworthy, universal truth: *The more you attempt to protect yourself from pain, the longer you continue behaving in a way that causes you the exact same pain you're trying to avoid.*

The only way out through the most difficult thoughts, emotions, and memories is through them. Even if you need to take medication to slow the down the fire, it doesn't matter: at some point, we all need to deal with our shit. Even if we have a clear-hearted vision of where we want our art to go, the strong sense of our inner truth, and support system in place, our destructive thoughts and the emotions that breed from them can and *will* sabotage us.

They'll gnaw at the edges of our idea until it fits in a safe little box.

They'll pump us full of sharp-edged worry until we can't untangle our true voice from the others anymore.

They'll scrape against our insecurities, whisper that our friends are lying.

They'll scratch at us until we run halfway across the world to escape them.

And they'll find us there, too.

YOUR FIRE, YOUR POWER

Luckily for us, creativity can help. Hundreds of studies spanning over three decades have analyzed the pattern between mental health and making art, and almost all of them found a significant reduction in negative emotions when a subject was actively creating. No one knows for sure what about making art is so therapeutic, but here's my best guess: When we set the intention to translate pain into a physical object, we move that pain out of our bodies as our project comes to life. By the time we've finished, we've dislodged one small pain point, one string of anxious thoughts and release it.

As creatives, we're in a unique position to understand and use our emotions instead of allowing them to burn through us haphazardly. We are *not* weak, weepy beings who are controlled by the tides of our emotional states, as society's stereotype paints us. Our emotions have never been an ocean. They are a flames of love, rage, sorrow, and they have the power to color our work in gold if we know what to do with them.

The way I see it, we have two options:

First, we can let our emotions set everything on fire. This is the option most people go with, for no other reason than it's all we've ever been taught to do. We've been told to just let a strong feeling run its course, to smash some dinner plates against a brick wall and forget about it. There's nothing inherently wrong with this advice, other than most of us assume this is where our work ends. In reality, your emotions are messengers that are trying to tell you that something is very, very wrong, and they will continue to come back in different forms until you fix what's broken. This is what I did those years surrounding my mom's death until the burn was so out of control that I could no longer use that pain to power my creativity. It snuffed it out instead.

Our second option is to accept the burning and build a safe space for it. Think about those barrel-sized fire pits at campsites; they're big enough to allow a decent size fire to run its course, but manageable enough to keep an eye on and put out if things start to get out of control. Our emotions are not going away, and because a lot of creatives tend to be sensitive, our fires burn with more intensity than most. To keep ourselves healthy and our work on course, we've gotta know how to build the pit when we need it. We've got to let our fire burn all the way through, sift through the ashes, and fix the gas leaks so it doesn't ignite so furiously the next time.

HOW TO BUILD YOUR FIRE:
FOUR STEPS TO USING EMOTIONS TO POWER YOUR ART

Step One: Watch for Smoke

The quickest way to let your fire loose in the wild is to pretend you aren't feeling whatever it is you're feeling. Denial will burn down your whole damn house if you let it. We can't let it.

It's essential that we do the hard work of examining our pain when it first surfaces instead of stuffing it away Be on the look out for triggers and pain points as you begin to work through your current project and this mapmaking process. You've cracked open your vulnerability to get here, and with that newfound openness often comes a flare of emotions. Pay close attention to your body whenever you're thinking about or working on your art: Do you feel tightness in your stomach? A lump in your throat? Headache? What's your general mood overall?

Keep a journal of any strange symptoms or thought patterns that seem to pop up whenever you're creating, or use the energy and mood tracker in the back of this book for easy tracking purposes. Often times, if we notice and acknowledge our emotions right from the get-go, they tend to dissipate on their own.

While you're paying close attention, remember to look back at the messages from your inner voice and stay the course as best you can.

Step Two: Build the Pit

If your emotions or negative thought patterns continue to press in, it's time to build your pit. Your pit is not a tool used to control your feelings, and we're never trying to tamp down the fire. Instead, consider it a safe space to allow the fire to run its course with minimal damage.

You'll need a pretty strong barrier to build this pit. When you feel like you're about to lose it, you don't have a lot of inner resources available to offer up to other people in your life. It's important to set some firm boundaries in place right now. Communicate clearly with your friends and family about what you need right now. Allow yourself more time for rest and self-care, and above all else, *keep creating.* Our greatest resistance lies before the work that will change us the most.

This work can bring up all sorts of sticky emotions and thought patterns, but that doesn't necessarily mean we should stop. As your feelings start to bubble over, acknowledge them. Recognize and name what you're feeling, and if you're up to it, free write in a journal to see if you can touch on the source of your discomfort.

Step Three: Let It Blaze

Sometimes a fire's gotta burn, even when we've done everything we can to figure out where the sparks are coming from. If you're here, your only job is to accept what is and to let it do its thing.

Each fire within you will burn differently. Rage may smolder before it transforms into a full-blown inferno. Anxiety fires may flicker in and out, and depression may blaze slowly and with persistence. If you've built a sturdy enough pit, there's a good chance that you and your art will be able to withstand the heat while suffering minimal damage. Don't be afraid to really dig deep here. Can you identify any worries, triggers, or stress that have been circulating through your mind recently? Has your art been a balm, or is it more like a match?

Step Four: Sift Through the Ash

The rain will come, the branches will burn through, and the fire will eventually die. The smoke around you will lift. You'll start to feel better, see clearer, but this isn't the time to call it in and jump straight back to work. If we want to be sure this particular fire doesn't ignite again, we have to take a closer look at what's been left behind.

As we sift through the ash with clearer vision, be sure to search through your energy and mood trackers, journals, and art. Look for an overarching pattern. Did anything unexpected, good or bad, happen around the same time the fire began? Were you creating something that triggered pain/anxiety/melancholy?

If you find that the work itself is bringing up too much pain to bear, there's almost always room to pivot without trashing everything you've done. It's totally okay to re-examine your map and choose a different emotional or mental landmark. You can always tweak what you have and keep moving toward your compass point.

You may also find now that the fire has burned off and some of the pain has dissipated you're ready to sprinkle the ash into your art. You may feel stronger, calmer, and settled enough to look at what's left of that pain and translate into something else. This, too, is okay. You're free to use whatever message you receive from these emotions in whichever way supports you as an artist and a human.

A few things to keep in mind as you're working through the aftermath of a fire:

• **Be ready for the next one.** Even after you've done the hard work of examining your most destructive thoughts and emotions, you may still experience the occasional flare-up. The fact is you are constantly changing, your art is always evolving, and as things shift, new triggers and traumas resurface. It's a little like Whack-A-Mole; just when you think you've squashed them, another one pops back up.

• **Extinguish shame.** No matter how many times your mental and emotional health take a hit, there's no place for shame. Allowing shame to infiltrate your heart is the equivalent to tossing a lit match into a puddle of gasoline: it's only going to make things worse. There's absolutely *no reason* why you should feel ashamed for struggling, especially when you're making every attempt to sort things out, but even when you haven't yet. You're human.

• **Fires are not required to fuel art.** The pervasive "tortured artist" stereotype that doesn't seem to want to die tells us that pain is art, and art is pain. It thrives off this twisted belief that we must suffer in order to create meaningful things, and that we should be grateful for our pain in return. This is, frankly, bullshit. There is no pain-threshold requirement to create. There's no contract that states your emotional agony must be present in all of your work. You're free to do with whatever insights your pain reveals to you, whether that includes writing them into a song or tucking them into the private space of your heart.

• **You come first, every time.** This work of examining our emotions is important, but it will never be as important as *you*. You're permitted to step back from anything that hurts you. You're allowed to care for yourself like you would for someone you love. In fact, it's required.

SOUND THE ALARM:
WHAT TO DO WHEN EVERYTHING'S
BURNING TO THE GROUND

There may come a time when the fire escapes the pit, when flames lick at the forest, and the whole damn thing starts to burn. No matter how doggedly you've worked through this guidebook, or how often you've gone to therapy, or how much self-care you've practiced, day in and out.

When you're in the midst of a full-blown panic attack, depressive episode, or explosive rage, it's downright impossible to think critically about the source of your emotions. In fact, it can be harmful. Your emotions are more forceful than your inner voice, and any insights you attempt while you're burning won't be a true reflection of who you are and which direction to take. Now's not the time to listen.

Now's the time for a hard reset.

The following checkpoint utilizes three methods recommended by psychologists to put a hard stop to destructive emotional episodes: acute physical action, distraction, and comfort. It also lists very specific choices under each section to take the brainstorming element out of it (less thinking for you when you don't have the energy for it). Feel free to add in other helpful action items in the boxes. Once you feel better again, go back to *Step #4: Sift Through the Ash* to analyze what happened and address any triggers.

Breathe, wild heart.

You've got this.

CHECKPOINT: YOUR FIRE EVACUATION PLAN

Directions: Use the *Stop (it), Drop (it), and Roll (with it)* plan below whenever you're struggling with intense emotional episodes. Circle one item under each section and then go do them, in order, right now. Do them as many times as you need until you start to feel better.

STOP (it)
Give yourself a hard physical reset

- snap a rubber band against your wrist
- take a 5 minute cold shower
- dunk your face in ice water for 30 seconds (yes, really)
- go for a ten-minute walk
- crank up a fan and let it blow on your face for 5 minutes
- press an ice pack on the back of your neck
- hold a plank for as long as you can

DROP (it)
Temporarily distract yourself from the emotion

- finish a coloring page (check out the emergency coloring sheets in the back of this book)
- do a crossword puzzle
- work on a simple craft project
- watch one episode of a light television show
- do a low-stress chore or yard work
- listen to a podcast
- read a chapter in your favorite book

ROLL (with it)
Seek out comfort as you roll through the last of it

- dim the lights and practice yogic breathing (deep breath in, exhale out)
- snuggle with a pet
- curl up in a soft blanket
- drink a cup of hot herbal tea
- take a hot bath
- reach out to a trusted friend or loved one
- take a nap

MAKE YOUR MAP: STEP #4

Go back to your map and draw in at least one fire pit somewhere along your path. You get to be creative here and place it wherever you see fit. Where are you most likely to experience strong emotions? Are there any landmarks or terrain on your map that can be triggering? Remember, this map is a visual representation of *your* individual, internal terrain. You're free to make whatever you want out of it!

Mapping Modification

Go back to a novel, poem, or movie you experienced in the past year that stirred a strong emotion within you. It can be any work of art as long as it wasn't made by you and it's in a medium that you actively *absorb* (so nothing that requires you to participate like cross-stitching, woodwork, etc.). Let that emotion bubble up. Allow yourself the time and space to explore why you think this piece of art struck you so deeply, and how it's affecting your current project. Draw a fire pit anywhere on your map as you see fit.

SIGNAL FOR HELP

Having a lover and friends who look at you as a true living, breathing entity,
one that is human but made of very fine and moist and magical things as well…
a lover and friends who support the criatura in you…
these are the people you are looking for.
They will be friends of your soul for life.
— Clarissa Pinkola Estés

On a drizzly Wednesday morning, I asked my dad if I could borrow his car to go to work. By Wednesday evening, I'd called off work, picked up three friends, and jumped the border between Michigan and Windsor, Canada with said car.

We scream-sang along to the tinny radio as I swerved through the streets of downtown Windsor, searching for a parking spot and place to eat. The adventure had been mostly unplanned, although we'd often discussed finding a tattoo parlor on Oulette Street that would pierce our bellybuttons without our mothers' permission. But on a whim and blessed with an unexpected half day in the spring of senior year, we'd decided to blow off everything to take the leap.

As the dashboard clock clicked toward three, my stomach began to sink. We were still trapped in traffic at the intersection of Windsor and the bridge back to Detroit, and my dad was minutes away from punching out at work. I'd probably get a few extra minutes while he waited for his ride, but it still wouldn't be enough.

I shut my eyes and imagined him standing on the stooped porch of his apartment building, arms crossed over his chest. I could already hear the bite in his voice as he reminded me of how irresponsible I was. And then there was the indefinite grounding that was sure to follow.

I squeezed the steering wheel until my knuckles turned white. My pinched thoughts began to spiral behind my eyelids, a tangle of *what ifs* and doomsdays statements about how I'd probably never see the outside of my bedroom again.

My friend, Catie, gently set her hand on top of mine. My fingers loosened. "You're going to be fine," she cooed. "We'll get the car back to your place, and everything will be okay, no matter *what* happens. *Breathe.*"

I opened my eyes and breathed. The traffic began to crawl forward.

As we raced toward home, my friend, Brianne, poked her head in between the front seats. "So you haven't heard from your dad yet, right?"

I shook my head. My pager (yes, pager) had been silent in my pocket all afternoon.

"So that means he's most likely not home yet, and you may still be able to make it! Just drop us all off at my house and I'll have my brother take Catie and Sarah home."

There was a murmur of agreement, and something like hope bloomed inside me. I was actually, maybe going to pull this off.

I shoved my friends out of the sedan with a haphazard wave and rocketed toward my dad's apartment complex. I threw the car into an empty parking spot, turned off the engine. Breathed.

There weren't any other cars in the lot.

I reached into my pocket and pulled out my pager. No messages.

I climbed the stairs and entered the apartment, only to find it empty, too. In the corner, the answering machine blinked. I tapped the button.

Hey, it's Dad. I'm going to be home a little late today, probably around five or six. See you soon.

Beep.

I sank into the couch. A giggle bubbled up in my throat, and then full-bellied laughter as the stress of the whole thing melted off me. I'd somehow, miraculously, done it.

The phone rang in its cradle. Sarah's warm voice greeted me when I picked up: "Hey, hey. Is everything okay over there?"

"Totally okay." I laughed. "My dad's not home yet."

"Thank god," she said. "So tell me, was it worth all the stress?"

Was it worth it? I sank back into the couch. Nothing had worked out exactly as planned. The tattoo parlor was closed, and the rain chilled us through our coats as we walked through the streets. And then there was the pressure, the endless scratching in the back of my mind begging me to *get home, get home, get home.*

But there was the white noise of the radio as we entered Canada, and the breathless laughter that fogged up the windows, flushed cheeks and stale drive-thru fries and the unalterable knowing that my friends had my back.

"I think so," I said.

She laughed. "Me, too."

INVITING OTHER PEOPLE INTO YOUR ADVENTURE

Although my friends and I had discussed the particulars of this adventure, I'd be lying if I told you it was a collective idea. In reality, I'd been the one to dream up this whole harebrained scheme, and I was the one who drove my dad's car straight across a foreign border (which he is well aware of now—sorry about that, Dad). But I wouldn't have been able to attempt the whole thing without them. Each one offered a specific strength on this journey, making the entire day both fun and unforgettable, and it still ranks up there as one of my fondest memories.

The truth is, we all need someone. Even the most single-minded, solitary endurance athletes and adventurers tend to stop at checkpoints to interact with other humans. Someone will be there to bring them water, another to cook them a homemade meal, more to cheer them on at the base of a mountain as they start their ascent.

Creatives, too, need other people. Although making art is a solitary experience— sometimes a long and arduous one—the outskirts of our lives and our work require the soft touch of support. When we're too stuck and stifled to care for ourselves, the best people in our lives will know exactly what to do to help us through it, whether that's providing comfort, cooking you a meal, reminding you to laugh, or imploring you to think beyond your own limitations. They'll fill you up with memories that just may show up in your work.

WHEN TO SIGNAL FOR HELP

In the previous chapters, we've explored our internal landscape: our dreams, traumas, one true voice, and emotional barriers. Now that you have a deeper understanding of what makes you, *you*, and can identify your own voice and emotions from what belongs to someone else, it's the perfect time to pivot toward the external aspects of creative life—including other people.

Here's why: Your process and project are still in a pretty fragile state right now. While you've found some clarity, generated ideas that feel good, and can distinguish your own inner guidance, there's a good chance you're still working through a bit of self-doubt. It takes a lot of courage to get up and give this a try again after a long drought, or a terrible rejection, or a life-altering trauma. Now that you know yourself a little better, this is the point where you can introduce other people for support while also knowing that their opinions won't lead you astray. You have the tools to take what you need from their words, and leave the rest behind. You know how to separate the megalomaniac wannabe artists from real friends, real artists who art itching to cheer you on.

Even if you're an intensely private introvert who enjoys spending a lot of time alone, you're still going to need some humans in your atmosphere. Let's face it: All art—whether you're drafting political thrillers or cross-stitching inspirational quotes— is an exploration on what it means to be human. Emotions, thought patterns, quests, friendships and broken hearts, it's *all* about living on this spinning rock in the sky. Inviting people into your process will do nothing less than remind you why you're making this thing in the first place.

On top of that, our interactions with other people have the potential to inspire us in new and unexpected ways. Here's an example: let's say you've started to put together the lyrics of a new song, but you can't seem to get the second verse just right. It sounds clunky, and the way the words string together doesn't make sense. You mention the problem to a friend, someone that always supported you while you were learning to play the guitar, and he mentions a songwriting workshop he attended that was super helpful. You pick up the book, untangle the verse, and suddenly, you have yourself a working song.

Creativity can't happen in a vacuum. Your most genuine characters, most thoughtful portraits are going to be inspired by the people and experiences that surround you. That being said, we still have to be extra careful about the people we choose to allow into our work at this point in the process. You need just the right people to push you, to comfort you, to strategize with you, to continue to inspire you.

So let's put out a smoke signal.

Let's find your people.

THE RESCUE SQUAD

Imagine this.

You are utterly and completely lost. Feel free to put in whichever backdrop is most terrifying for you, personally, whether it's a forest or a desert or a room that looks like something straight out of *Saw*. The point is: You have no idea where you are and you don't know how to get out.

What kind of people do you want by your side?

Maybe your childhood BFF's name popped into your head, or maybe it was your mom's, or your aunt's, or your favorite teacher's. It's inevitable that your brain will rollercoaster toward the most familiar and knowable right off the bat, especially when you're lonely and vulnerable.

But now's the time to look outside of what we already have and be brave enough to think about what we actually need. If you want to make beautiful/silly/soulful/gut-wrenching things in the world, we need the kind of people that align with our highest intentions.

So let's try again. You're lost, you're scared. Your heartbeat's roaring in your ears. Miraculously, you find a single match in your pocket. You start a fire and signal for help.

What kind of people do you want on your rescue squad to get you through this?

Every creative is unique, and we all need different people at different points in our lives, but time and time again, I've found myself reaching for someone who aligns with one of these four archetypes when I'm struggling.

The Medic

Traits: *Nurturing, Hopeful, Helpful*

You can recognize a Medic by the look on their face when you're telling them a story. They'll often look extremely worried when something bad happens to you or your characters, even if you both know the whole ordeal has a happy ending. It's not that these gentle souls are worriers—they're really warriors in the most humanitarian sense of the word. Medics are the people who tend to our wounds when we've been cut by stinging rejections. They're our human IVs when we need a lifeline and the stitches that hold our insides together. These are the people who are natural nurturers who will patch you up with your favorite cookies or a super sweet text so you can keep going.

The Observer

Traits: *Logical, Analytical, Problem-solver*

That friend who always has the quickest comeback? The one who remembers every story you've ever told *and* isn't afraid to correct you on it when you get your own facts twisted? That would be your Observer. These are the people who see things that you may miss, who are almost always capable of logic-ing their way out of the most difficult situations. The Observer in your life may act as your critique partner or a friend who keeps you in check, but either way, they're there to (gently, but firmly) point out the gaping plot holes in your work or the weak spot you have for toxic people. All for the better, wild heart.

The Explorer

Traits: *Adventurous, Ballsy, Rebellious*

You can identify an Explorer by the way they make you feel, which is usually somewhere between thrilled and freaking terrified. They don't necessarily think the rules apply to them, and while this can rub some people the wrong way, this kind of energy is sure to ramp you up and deliver a much-needed confidence boost. The Explorer is who I always go to after a string of tough rejections, as they're the first to tell me, "So what? Who says you can't do that with your writing? Screw 'em." Through their plucky spirit, an Explorer will hold your hand and help you cross the river, even if you're terrified of drowning. They know when you're ready to leap, even when you don't yet.

The Elder

Traits: *Intuitive, Wise, Visionary*

Where the Explorer pushes you to go wider, the Elder asks you to go deeper. This person is your natural intuitive, counselor, and always seems to be able to say the right thing at the right time. The Elder will help you untangle any unhealthy thought patterns behind your artistic choices, while prodding you to finally look at the things you've been missing. They're the dreamers, the visionaries, and they'll always help you see the long-game when it comes to your own ambitions.

When you're brainstorming who could fit these archetypes in your life, it's important to stay flexible and open-minded. For one thing, each and every project you take on will need a different set of eyes, a different set of ears, and a different voice to remind you of your vision *and* your blind spots. You'll find that for one painting you may really lean on an Elder to help you sort through the meaning behind your piece, but for a series of sketches you may need an Explorer to push you to try something new.

It's also important to recognize that people are just as fluid as art. You may need one certain Explorer for one novel, but a different Explorer for an essay you're trying to piece together. And don't discount the people who don't necessarily fit these molds. There are many people in my life who don't have a direct influence over my creative process, but who are still important for other reasons. They make me laugh, they help me take myself less seriously, they share a bond with me over *Teen Mom* and stupidly expensive eyeshadow palettes. What I'm saying is: Don't kick everyone out if they don't fit the mold, okay?

LOCATING A MISSING SQUAD MEMBER

At the following checkpoint, we'll spend some time envisioning our rescue squad, but what if you just can't think of someone for a specific archetype? Let's say you've got an Explorer, a Medic, an Observer, but…your Elder seems to be MIA. No matter how long you rack your brain, you can't identify anyone in your life who would fit that particular role. In that case, here are a few tips to finding the people you need if they aren't in your life just yet:

- **Look through a longer lens.** It's completely possible that you *do* have who you need, but you haven't been thinking of them in that way. Don't be afraid to talk to other people in your inner circle and ask them who they rely on for advice, or nurturing, or solid kick in the ass. It's possible that this person belongs to your circle too, and you haven't been able to see them in this lens before. Maybe your goofy next-door neighbor actually spits some decent wisdom when it comes to creativity and you hadn't really noticed it before. Maybe your grandpa *is* kind of a badass button-pusher, considering he checked himself out of his nursing home and took a cab to Vegas. Pay attention. You may be pleasantly surprised.

- **Send your signal even wider.** If you're having trouble coming up with someone, cast your signal a little wider. There are millions of people all over the globe that share your same interests and would be more than willing to talk creativity with you. Consider looking into the artist and writer communities on Twitter and Instagram. I've met some of my closest friends and most brilliant critique partners by participating in contests with other writers on Twitter, and those people have definitely helped me fill gaps in my work again and again.

- **Grab some momentum and roll with it.** There's a quote from Rumi that says, "Stop acting so small. You are the universe in ecstatic motion." What I've always taken this to mean is that even our smallest, simplest efforts toward a goal make ripples, and that those ripples have the potential to create outcomes that we haven't even dreamed of yet. The best way to find what you need is to just get started anyway. Use what you have and take a leap of faith as you start your project, and allow the pieces to fall in place at the right time. You may find that you didn't actually need that Elder to start with at all, but the right one appeared at the end when you needed her most. Keep going, and watch who shows up to fill in the empty spaces.

HOW TO ASK FOR SUPPORT

Once you have a clear idea of who at least a few of your squad members could be, it's time to reach out for support. If you're used to flying solo, this can be pretty intimidating at first, but don't let your fear-voice take the reigns, *especially* at this critical point in your creative recovery. Remind yourself that all of your anxieties surrounding rejection or asking for help are not your true voice. They don't represent what you need or what kind of creative you strive to be.

When you ask for support, keep it simple. No need to inform someone that they're now your bonafide Medic and their new duties include bringing you cookies on the regular. You've already done—and will continue to do at the next checkpoint—the work of figuring out how they could fit into your support system. You already *know* they're naturally nurturing so you don't need to assign them responsibilities (not to mention it's rude). When you ask for support, point out all of their qualities that made you think of them. For example: *I've always admired how caring you are toward your friends. You've also always offered me kind words when I really needed it. Would you mind if I emailed you some time to talk about this project I'm working on? It's been pretty tough, but I feel like I can trust you.*

Keep it simple, and don't put pressure on them to dig you out of your own hole. They're there to provide tools to help you be successful. They aren't there to inhale all of your anxieties and cling to you while you combust. It's important to approach this sacred relationship with gratitude instead of assumptions and expectations. Any support you receive should be deeply respected.

This work is primarily yours. It's up to you to discern when you need an extra dose of support from your squad and when its time to figure your way out on your own.

RESPONDING TO SOMEONE ELSE'S SIGNAL

We've talked a lot about how our rescue squad can help us, but it's equally important to give of ourselves to the people in our lives. Your rescue squad will pull you from the sharpest edges of yourself, but it's your responsibility as a human to return the favor. You may find that when you do, your own confidence and creativity increase, and that you feel fastened to a bigger purpose outside of your own internal monologue. Giving back to others is what keeps us soft, keeps us real, and reminds us that connection is the purpose of creating in the first place.

CHECKPOINT: MAKE YOUR RESCUE SQUAD KIT

Directions: Fill in the four character outlines below with details about each member of your rescue squad. Start by sketching an image or doodling about your archetype in the blank box. If you already know who you'd like to tap for extra support, feel free to fill in more specifics about how this person could be helpful during this project. Note: the goal of this activity is not to share it with them, but for your own self-awareness. By getting clear on what you need, you'll be able to recognize who could help and when, and when it's time to work through something on your own.

The Medic	The Observer	The Explorer	The Elder
I know I need to reach out when I've been feeling _____ for _____ days.	I know I need to reach out when I've been feeling _____ for _____ days.	I know I need to reach out when I've been feeling _____ for _____ days.	I know I need to reach out when I've been feeling _____ for _____ days.
Some words or phrases I say to myself when I'm feeling this way are:	Some words or phrases I say to myself when I'm feeling this way are:	Some words or phrases I say to myself when I'm feeling this way are:	Some words or phrases I say to myself when I'm feeling this way are:
Three specific ways the Medic can help right now are: • • •	Three specific ways the Observer can help right now are: • • •	Three specific ways the Explorer can help right now are: • • •	Three specific ways the Elder can help right now are: • • •

MAKE YOUR MAP: STEP #5

Cut out or draw the small character sketches and place them on your map. If you're feeling extra creative, you can even place them near the landmarks that remind you of them. You can also draw in any sort of dangerous terrain—cliffs, caves, canyons, etc.— and label each one with the emotions you identified in the chart, or you can place them by a fire pit you drew in the last activity. Be sure to keep your squad members close by so they can help lift you out if you find yourself in danger.

Mapping Modification

If you're having a hard time putting together your squad or asking for help, go ahead and start off with anyone you trust, even if you're not sure they fit into one of the four archetypes. And don't even worry if you don't have four yet! What's most important now is that you can lean on someone so you can keep moving forward.

LISTEN FOR THE RIVER

When you do things from your soul, you feel a river moving in you, a joy.
— Rumi

I didn't bring a notebook or a pen to my last creative writing class in college. I showed up empty-handed and prepared to absorb my professor's parting advice before he let all of us out for summer break.

The class had been enjoyable enough, the assignments interesting enough, but I still found myself bored. I'd written a parade of stories on the same topics I always tended to wander toward in these sort of classes: white-hot childhood trauma, damp melancholy, and bitter endings. By the time I sank into my seat for the last time, I was more than ready to pack the pens away and settle into the sunshine.

"All right then!" Dr. Lipton said, clapping. "Last class, last assignment."

Last assignment?

The room grew quiet as we all turned the words over in our head. A guy named Michael raised his hand. "So, you're giving us an assignment? On the last day of class?"

But Dr. Lipton didn't answer. He hovered over each desk, passing out a single sheet of paper and a pen to each of us. I glanced at the title: *The Necessity of Joy.* Beneath it, there was this prompt:

This semester, we've mined past traumatic events for the raw materials that would become your stories. We've discussed how to use personal experiences with anger, rage, and sadness to create a broader narrative. For our last assignment, I'd like for you to consider this statement: "Joy is more essential to writing than any other emotion." Please state your opinion, followed by a short example of how joy has/will make you a better writer.

I stared at the words, forcing my brain to come up with something, *anything*, that would hand me the A in this class I knew I deserved. I combed through my memories, but they scrabbled across my mind like autumn leaves in a parking lot. I couldn't catch them, and the ones I did were dried out and faded.

I couldn't remember the last time I'd felt *joy*. Happiness? sure. A general sense of well-being? Okay. But joy? It was possible I'd never experienced it at all.

The clock wound down. In the final moments of the hour, I scribbled down the only truth that I could come up with, and it was this:

No, writers don't need to experience joy to be great. Some of the greatest writers were depressed, and most of the most prominent American novels deal with heavy subject matter. Like this writers, I also explore darker subject matter in my work and I'm no less happy for it.

I handed Dr. Lipton the paper and started toward the door. "Andrea, wait," he called. "One last thing."

I gritted my teeth and turned back. I was more than done with this subject matter. I didn't want to his his argument for the necessity of joy; I wasn't interested in another debate.

"Do me a favor this summer, okay?" he said, folding my paper back into my hand. "Find some joy, even just a little bit, even if it seems ridiculous. And once you do, sit down and write something while you feel that way."

I lifted an eyebrow. "Is that everything?"

"Yes, it really is," he said.

JOY IS A RIVER

After the class ended, I attempted Dr. Lipton's bonus assignment. I wish I could tell you that it was successful, that I found a sliver of joy in the midst of my summer, but I can't say with certainty that I did. There was plenty of happiness, but with it came the looming pressure of life after graduation. I was proud of everything I'd accomplished, but I recognized I had fought tooth-and-nail to work double shifts and finish school. The whole thing wasn't exactly puppies and rainbows.

I only started to recognize and appreciate joy when I actively sought it. This may seem counterintuitive to society's beliefs about what makes a "joyful" experience, but for some of us, it requires a little more effort. Some of us more anxiety-ridden types have to consciously pause and listen for it.

When you're lost in the woods, most avid explorers agree that a similar sort of pause is required to find your way. Only then can you listen for the rush of moving water. In order to get out, you have to continue to pause and listen, again and again, until you discover the source of the sound and follow it. You *need* to find that water. Not only is it essential for your biological survival, you will almost always find some sort of civilization built upon it if you travel far enough.

Joy, too, will lead you out of the woods if you know how to listen for it.

THE NECESSITY OF JOY

The first three chapters of this section focused on honing our vision and getting crystal-clear on the steps we need to take to get there. The previous two chapters touched on our emotions as messengers, how to use them to build a support system, and what to do when they create an obstacle on our path. So far, we've only discussed our negative emotions and thought patterns, but to stop there would only address half of the picture. If our goal is to make a map of our *whole* internal, creative life then we have to have conversation around the good stuff, too. We've gotta talk about joy.

So, what *is* joy?

Merriam-Webster defines it as "a feeling of great pleasure and happiness." And while that's a good start, it doesn't quite do it justice. Joy is a combination of delight plus a dash of surprise. It's the warmth of happiness injected with a dose of the unexpected. We often associate it with "big" moments—weddings, births, career accomplishments—but that has more to do with our expectation than it does with joy. We think we should feel joyous in these circumstances, and so we associate that hope with the ideation of joy, but that doesn't mean we're actually *feeling* it. There have been many major moments in my life where I've felt anything but joyous, and yet I still describe them as such in my memories.

On top of all that, joy can only be accessed through the present moment. Think about it: It's damn near impossible to be joyous when your mind is crashing through the future, worrying about paying next month's rent, or re-playing the time you crashed your bike and sprained your wrist. We can only truly feel it when we're relaxed in the here and delighted by what's happening in the now.

Up until this point, we've discussed all of the obstacles you may face as you work on your art, but we've yet talked about tools and methods to help you escape. This is where joy comes in. While destructive emotions are roadblocks, joy is what clears the path. You have to calm the emotions that undo you, you *also* have to actively seek out the ones that make you.

This is how you get out.

Not by waiting to be rescued.

Not by waiting for another wildfire to pass.

By listening, again and again, for the river.

WHY ARTISTS HAVE A HARD TIME ACCEPTING JOY

Every creative I know wants to feel good. We all want to enjoy our work, feel satisfied with our lives, and bliss out at least every once in awhile. But we often have a harder time both accepting joy and actively seeking it out for a number of reasons.

- **Pollution of thought.** There are a lot of messed up beliefs surrounding joy and pleasure in our society. We've been taught that joy is a luxury, a product of our good behavior and right choices. If we're lucky. Sometimes we'll be rewarded with joy and other times, not so much. It's fickle like that.

  This line of thinking is false and damaging. Experiencing joy is a necessary part of being human. It's not a reward for on point behavior, or a prize, or something bestowed upon us by the big man in the sky. It's not wild and irrational. Joy, like all other emotions, is accessible to us. We have the power to create an environment where it can flow naturally.

  Often times creatives are drilled with the message that they're outsiders, that they're strange and probably even a bit self-centered for wanting to make art instead of getting a "real job." Subconsciously, we absorb the idea that because we haven't followed the rules, we don't deserve the prize. We play this fake, zero-sum game that tells us we *chose* this, so we have to accept that joy may not follow.

- **Swimming upstream.** Because we've been lambasted for taking a different path, we also subconsciously believe that we have to work ourselves into the grave in the name of the dream. To prove that we're not selfish, lazy "hippies" who don't want to work, we swim like hell against the current. We figure that if we work hard enough, finally get that book published or snag that gallery spot, that will prove something to the rest of them. We'll finally be worthy of pursuing what we love, and then *maybe*, we'll earn the joy our work brings us.

  Again, this is damaging bullshit. Say it again with me: *You deserve to experience joy because you exist, and nothing more.*

- **Fear of drowning.** We already know a lot of us are sensitive to the ebb and flow of emotions. Many of us have been burned by feelings that have led us astray before, or have been deeply disappointed when our happiness waned despite our best efforts to hang on to it. That fear of losing something so good can be enough to stop just short of the riverbank. We tell ourselves that this is good enough, we're close enough to hear it, we don't need to dip our toes in. It's safer to pull back than it is to go all the way under, only to be crushed when we lose the river again.

WHAT HAPPENS TO YOUR ART WHEN YOU PURSUE JOY: AN EXAMPLE

Eventually, I completed Dr. Lipton's assignment.

Five years after graduation, I sat down to attempt my first book. As always, my ideas had drifted toward the morose, and my outline was punctuated with murders and missing persons and a constellation of other traumas. Truth be told, I hadn't been exactly joyous when I'd worked out the plot. In fact, I hadn't even been anywhere near happy the past couple of years. The only reason I had decided to sit down and write was because I was desperate to claw my way out of my own skin for a little while.

I was typing one day in mid-April when my husband, Matt, rushed into the bedroom. "Hey, you gotta look outside," he said breathlessly, and bolted toward the back porch. I followed him, only to find snowflakes splattered across the windows.

I pulled open the door and stepped outside. The temperature had dipped just low enough to make the spring drizzle freeze over, and now fat, wet snowflakes littered the patio in place of cotton blossoms.

Matt stuck out his tongue, and I did, too. My stomach bubbled up with delight as we spun, open-armed, under the purple-bellied clouds and let spring snow drift into our mouths. It was a quite moment, insignificant, even, except it changed everything.

I went back to my computer, still buzzing, and began to type out a scene. In the outline version, there was supposed to be a shock of pain as the main character realized her friend had betrayed her. Instead, I wrote her softer. Her pain was still there, but so was the sweet sense of longing for their friendship as she walked home in the snow. She became more that just pain on the page; she became complicated and technicolored and *human.*

And so did I.

FOLLOWING THE RIVER

While we can't control when joy will show up, we *can* create the best possible environment for it when it does. Here are a few tips that will help you calm your mind, listen to your heart, and follow that river straight out of the woods.

- **Take conscious pauses.** Since joy's only available in the present moment, we have to make continual efforts to bring our attention back here, again and again. Be sure to build in a conscious break or two into your day to just sit, relax, and bask in where you are, now.

- **Tamp down your expectations.** The path to disappointment is paved with expectations, and that's exactly where you'll find yourself if you're expecting joy to pop up in certain places. Remember, joy is delight and surprise. Your best bet to experiencing it is to not expect it at all.

- **Listen closely.** Oftentimes our inner voice has a lot to say about what truly makes us happy. Take time to connect with that voice regularly and listen to what it tells you, even if the advice doesn't make sense at first. For example, my inner voice constantly nudges me toward exercise when I'm feeling drained, which…going to be honest here, is not the first thing that comes to mind when I think of joy. But every time I go out and do it, I *do* find joy—I'm happy when my body feels strong and being outside recharges me like nothing else. Listen closely and let yourself be surprised.

- **Actively pursue pleasure.** It's going to be tough to find joy while you're scrubbing the bathroom floor (unless you love that sort of thing, then go, you!). Think of three things that feel like pure *pleasure* to you, and give it your best effort to do them as often as possible.

I want you to treat this task with the same seriousness as you did when dealing with more difficult thoughts and emotions. We're retraining ourselves to think of joy as a necessity, not a privilege, and it's going to take the same level of commitment to rewrite this collective story.

Follow that river and cling to its banks. Don't let go.

Your art and your heart depend on it.

CHECKPOINT: RIVERBED JOY TRACKER

Directions: Below you'll find the image of an empty riverbed. Beside it, there are four "rocks," or Tetris-shaped pieces. In the sections, write one activity that brings you pleasure to represent each one. If you're having trouble thinking of some, check out the following prompts to get you started:

- *When I'm absolutely drained, all I want to do is _____.*
- *When I daydream about my future, I'm always _____.*
- *I always lose track of time when I _____.*

After you've written down your five activities on the rocks, you can track how often you do them with this fun puzzle-like tracker. *There's no order or amount you need to do them in, no limits on which kinds of rocks need to fill up the riverbed.* Your only goal is to get the rocks to *fit together* within the tracker, much like Tetris pieces fit together on a game board. When you fill it up, it's simple to trace it and do it again in your bullet journal or planner.

FOLLOW THE RIVER
track your joy

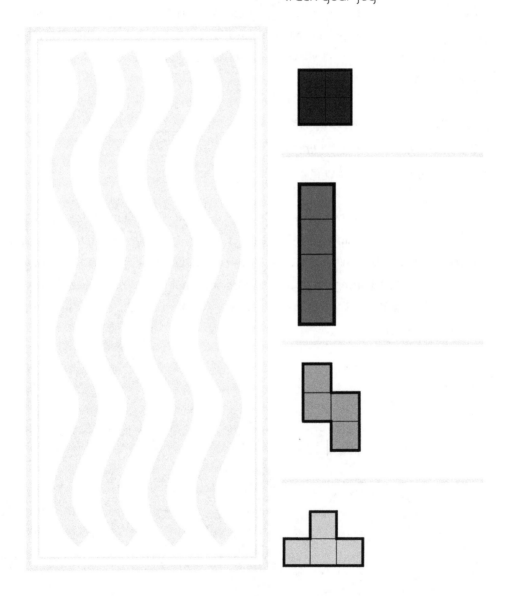

MAKE YOUR MAP: STEP #6

It's finally time to draw your river running through your map. Again, this is totally in your hands. It can be wide and rocky, or more of a slow-moving stream. You can draw it alongside your path, or it can show up on the opposite side of the map. The only requirement is that it has a clear end point out of the thick of it because *that*'s where we're headed. Feel free to add in words or images that bring you joy throughout the river.

Mapping Modification

We're going to rely on other media again here to help you through this activity. If you're having trouble coming up with people, places, or things that bring you joy, research your favorite media. Take a closer look at the novels, movies, music, and TV shows that make you feel good. What elements within them make you joyful? Which of those elements can you bring into your project?

FIND YOUR SHELTER

In limits, there is freedom. Creativity thrives within structure. — Julia Cameron

On a whim, I booked a to New Orleans just before hurricane season rolled in. I'd always been drawn to the city's folklore, and I was eager to explore the mythology of ghosts, voodoo, and witchcraft. My best friend, Keri, and I signed up for a slightly cheesy ghost tour of the French Quarter on the first night.

Our guide arrived wearing Jordans and a pair of clear-framed glasses. He was boisterous as we wove through the cobblestone streets, cheerfully recalling New Orlean's gritty history. We hustled under flickering hurricane lamps to keep up until he stopped abruptly in front of a shadowy mansion. He wove a story of a sultan who had immigrated to New Orleans. Despite all his riches, he wasn't able to save himself from his brother's wrath. He, and all of the women who loved him, were murdered inside that house.

The guide continued, telling more stories about the barred windows, mysterious suicides, and tragic murders. "New Orleans, you see, was founded on ancient Native American burial ground," he boomed, shoving his glasses up his nose. "The Natives told the French not to colonize this land, not only because, well, it was *their* land, but because they believed the land was cursed. And, of course, we didn't listen. So you see, we populated the land. We built on the bayou, and we've been paying for it ever since. Disease, famine, hurricanes, death, and a magnanimous amount of bad, bad luck have plagued New Orleans ever since, forcing us to rebuild again and again."

I glanced at the pockmarked streets and candlelight spilling from shopfronts. Knots of tourists wafted toward cramped oyster houses and bars. It was hard to imagine what this had looked like even ten years ago while the city was still rebuilding after Katrina.

All of these shops had surely folded in on themselves, their window fronts punctured by windswept debris. Hurricane lamps had been crushed, bulbs smashed, the entire city left in sweltering darkness.

Everything around me had seemed so firm, so ancient, rooted in its history. And yet, it had been ravaged and rebuilt, again and again. The city was vibrant and lush, but the foundation just beneath was as fragile as a fresh beignet.

"I'm sure they'll have to build again one day," Keri whispered.

The blistering truth settled into me. One day, this street will be barren and battered again. Lamps will shatter, shops will collapse, homes will flood.

The city will rise again from the water, people will return, lives will restart.

But the foundation will always be shaky.

OWNING YOUR GROUND

Whether New Orlean's terrible luck is because of its proximity to the sea or due to an ancient curse, it's safe to say that it wasn't constructed on a solid foundation. That decision will continue to affect it for as long as the coastline still exists.

The decision to set up camp while you're in the woods should be considered with the same level of seriousness. It's critical that the foundation you choose is level, above water, firm, and capable of holding your body weight. It needs to be inconspicuous, and most important, it needs to be all yours. Imagine waking to find a seriously pissed off grizzly who was expecting to find his spot vacant.

You can't build on ground that was never yours to begin with.

The creative, too, needs a solid foundation from which to build a flourishing life, but it must be of their own conscious making. We have to search with discernment. We have to know ourselves well enough to choose a foundation that will last much longer than a week, a year, even ten years. We need to pick soil firm enough—but also rich enough—to nurture the habits, routines, and boundaries we must put into place.

It's on this ground, this foundation, that we can build a shelter that's both safe and essential to our creative life. It's here that we'll develop the daily procedures that will carry us forward.

This is where we get out of the woods.

OUR PHYSICAL BODY:
THE FOUNDATION OF CREATIVE HEALTH

Throughout this book, we've addressed mental and emotional health, and pinpointed how to increase our joy. But to truly reach our creative potential, we can't discount the role of our physical body.

A quick Google search on the connection between mental health, emotions, and creativity produces hundreds of thousands of research abstracts, summarized studies, blog posts, and mainstream news articles. The relationship between our physical bodies and creativity, though? That's a little harder to find.

The good news is that seems to be changing. A recent study put this question to the test: *Can exercise increase creativity in a measurable way?*[*] During the study, participants completed Guilford's alternate uses (GAU) test of creative divergent thinking before and after aerobic exercises. The results shows that all participants demonstrated higher-level, more innovative thinking immediately following exercise. Since then, more studies have been conducted on the link between healthy living and creativity. As recently reported in *The New York Times*, another study proved that "when we exercise, far-flung parts of our bodies apparently communicate with each other."[**] Researchers speculate that while we're working out our internal organs—our brain included—have the chance to check in with each other, balance each other, and deliver insights that we wouldn't have otherwise been able to receive.

Another way our creativity gets a boost is through the foods we eat. Scientists have always hypothesized that certain foods could actually enhance creativity, but they've just recently been able to pinpoint how. Dr. Gomez-Pinilla, a biologist who studies the effects of nutrition on the aging body, has found consuming more raw fruits and vegetables increases creative thinking due to the boost of inflammation-fighting flavonoids that you get with each serving.

Look, I'm sure this isn't the first time you've heard exercise and healthy eating are good for you. I'm not here to wag a finger at you and tell you to replace all your meals with kale. Ultimately, *you* know your own body best, and you know what it needs to function, and only you can identify what you need for a solid foundation. My only goal is to make the connection between our bodies and our creative output clearer. When you find yourself stuck, it often takes an all-encompassing, brave-hearted effort to break free and find our flow. Caring for our physical body can help.

* Oppezzo, Mary. 2014. *The positive effect of walking on creativity.* https://psycnet.apa.org/buy/2014-14435-001

** Reynolds, Gretchen. 2018. *The Mysterious Inner World of Exercise.* https://www.nytimes.com/2018/01/24/well/move/the-mysterious-interior-world-of-exercise.html

LAYING THE GROUNDWORK:
HOW TO NOURISH YOUR BODY AS A CREATIVE

While the following tips can work for anyone, they specifically apply to creatives who are actively working on their art. Certain ailments and aches tend to pop up during periods of intense focus or emotional and mental strain, and these are a few things that can help your body to rise to the occasion.

- **Watch out for rocks:** Every time you sit down to create, take a quick pause to check in with your body. Does anything feel sharp or pinched? Does your stomach feel uneven? The goal is just to observe. When you've finished your project for the day, check back in with your body. Has anything changed? Is it better or worse? Take note.

  Oftentimes our bodies will hold onto stress and other emotions in the form of sore muscles, stomach pain, headaches, or something else entirely. By paying attention to your body as you create, you can get a better sense of how that process is impacting you as a whole.

- **Smooth out the soil.** I tend to hold all of my stress in my neck and back. When I've been grinding for too long without rest, my upper back will usually start screaming at me until I put the laptop down. Your body, too, probably has its own tells in the form or acute aches and pains. After you've noticed when and where they pop up, be sure to listen to what they're saying and then care for yourself. Smooth out those muscle knots. Take a hot bath. Sleep. Give yourself a pause so your body can find its equilibrium again. Remember, we're working on setting a strong, level foundation before we build. Balance is necessary.

- **Clear it out. No** one expects you to live off of green juice while you're working on your art. And I am surely not the one to tell you to lay off the M&Ms as I have a collection of all flavors and sizes currently hanging out in my cupboard. What does help, though, is identifying a few foods that regularly bring your energy down. For me, that's almost all dairy. It makes me feel sick, sluggish, and foggy-headed. I try to stay away from it as much as I can, but especially when I'm actively creating. Pay attention to your body as you take in meals. What slows you down? Makes you feel great? Less of the former, more of the latter.

- **Do the work and dig.** Finally, some exercise can do wonders for your work, your body, and your mental health. When I'm running regularly, I'm clearer, more confident, and have the energy to tackle whatever obstacle I bump up against in my projects. My art is infinitely better and requirers fewer revisions. So, how about you? How do you like to move your body and when can you do it? It's okay to start in small batches—a ten minute walk, fifteen minutes of yoga—as long as it challenges you. And if physical exercise isn't available to you, not to worry. You can still use any of the activities in the appendix (especially the coloring pages) to help you gain clarity.

BUILDING A STRUCTURE: SCHEDULING IN PHYSICAL, MENTAL, AND EMOTIONAL HEALTH

Without fail, at the end of almost every workshop I've been a part of, someone asks this question:

Where do you find the time to write?

In the past I've rambled on about how to get up early, or how my noise-canceling headphones have saved me, or how I set my notebook out the night before. But after almost a decade of writing on the regular with deadlines that have to be met, I've realized that all the tips and tricks in the world aren't going to do anything for me if I'm not taking care of my physical, emotional, and mental needs first.

Here's why: I could buy a sunlight-stimulating alarm clock to gently prod me out of sleep at 5 AM, and sure, those extra pre-dawn hours will give me more time to create. *But anything that I write is will still be a manifestation of how well my needs have been met.* If my body aches, or I've been struggling with an anxiety spiral, or I'm still grieving over my dog dying, it's going to show up in how I do my work. And yes, art can help you process some of this stuff, but it also has the potential to trip up your original vision for your project. We can't afford that right now. Not when we're so close to the edge of the forest.

Now, I build my life around health and wellbeing before anything else. Even my creative work.

This is a hard idea to settle into at first. Creatives are some of the busiest people I know, always trying to pull water from the rock of their overpacked schedules. But still, I question how much of our time we devote to things that are not nearly as critical as we originally thought. And I often wonder how much time we'd free up if we felt the best we possibly could.

Using what we know now about how we operate physically, mentally, and emotionally, we're going to build a new structure from the ground up. We'll take some data on ourselves, and set up routines that will keep us focused, shelter us, and sustain us for the long trip home.

CHECKPOINT: SETTING UP CAMP

Directions: In each section below, you'll find an activity and/or tracker for you to fill out as you build your new structure. Do them in order, as one builds on the other. When you're finished, feel free to write down your new schedule and routines into a planner, bullet journal, calendar, or anything else you may use.

COLLECT MATERIALS

Use the trackers below to observe when you feel best throughout a typical day. Shade in the hours you've slept. Then choose a color to represent low energy, average energy, and high energy, and color in each hour. You can do this once, or over several days to look for a pattern.

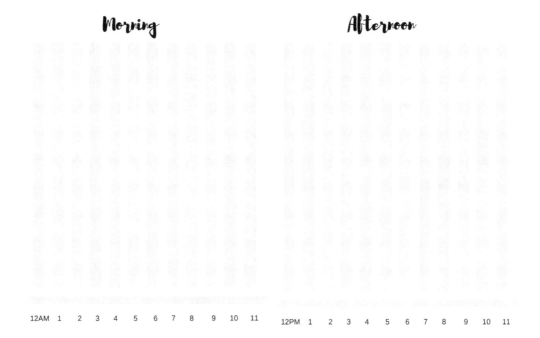

Morning

Afternoon

12AM 1 2 3 4 5 6 7 8 9 10 11   12PM 1 2 3 4 5 6 7 8 9 10 11

SET UP SHELTER

First, take a look at those "low energy" blocks. These are the times you must take care of yourself in any way you need. Don't try to work on your art here. Take a look at the seven blocks below representing a typical week and block off time here to exercise, nap, journal, snuggle with your pet, or anything else that lifts your energy during typical low energy times.

Weekly

AM

PM

| Monday | Tuesday | Wednesday | Thursday | Friday | Saturday | Sunday |

BUILD THE BASICS

Now look at the "average energy" blocks in your first tracker. We're going to reserve these for all of the stuff you have to do: grocery shopping, emails, errands, etc. Color in the chunks of time you'll set aside for this type of work.

Weekly

| Monday | Tuesday | Wednesday | Thursday | Friday | Saturday | Sunday |

RECHARGE AND PLAN YOUR NEXT MOVE

Last, let's focus on the hours you've identified as "high-energy." We're going to reserve as many of these as possible for creative work only. Color in the chunks of time that you'll devote to making art.

PUTTING IT ALL TOGETHER

Take what you've learned about yourself and apply it to any planner or calendar that works best for you. It helps to repeat this exploration every few months to see if your energy has changed and adjust your schedule accordingly.

MAKE YOUR MAP: STEP #7

Your map is almost complete, wild heart. The only thing left to do is mark your exit. Wherever you see fit, draw a symbol on the outside of the forest to identify your newfound freedom. This could be as simple as a star, or an actual image of you standing on the other side. Make sure to hang onto your map, and your schedule tracking sheets, even after you've finished the work you've started here. Your map now serves as a visual representation of your creative process for this project. It's there to remind you that you can always, always find your way out of the darkness, again and again, no matter how often you lose your way while making your art.

Mapping Modification

There's only one modification for this one. It's this: Take it as slow as you need to. If you haven't finished your map, are still missing pieces, or just don't feel done with figuring out your project yet, that is more than okay. Take it slow. Listen. You'll know when it's time to make your exit.

INTERLUDE

THE LIGHT

The river weaves through the trees. The canopy is so thick that it feels like night has swallowed up the forest. You can't even remember the last time you saw even an errant streak of sunlight.

But you've moved on anyway.

You've taken steps in the right direction, day after day, with blistering faith.

You've paid close attention to the woods around you, and used your landmarks to show you the way forward.

You've listened to your own true north when you were scared.

You've harnessed wildfires to keep you calm, sent smoke signals for help, and you've followed the river's edge to this place, here and now.

You've allowed yourself the soft blanket of shelter to recharge and strategize, and you've gotten up and moved once again.

The trees begin to wane from the riverbank. They thin as you push forward. In the distance, you can see the shape of a sloped roof, and then a house, and then more houses.

Sunlight settles on your shoulders like a fine dust.

You run.

You burst through the forest and race into the sweeping grass. You close your eyes, tip your head toward the sky, and let the sun warm you once again.

PART THREE

TIPS, TRICKS, AND STRATEGIES
FOR WHEN YOU START TO
FEEL STUCK AGAIN

START FROM YOUR DESTINATION

There's a path cut for us, a destination mapped out.
Everyone ends up where they're meant to be,
and how they got there doesn't really matter.
— Pattie Boyd

Not all creatives are alike, but there are a few principles that help us all stay stay the course:

We all need to feel heard.

We need to create something in order not to destroy ourselves.

We need a solid, yet flexible structure to build our lives around in order to manifest the greatest version of our creativity.

While the chapters in this book focus on systematically building healthy creative life, I recognize that we also experience things in our own way. I know we can't always do everything in the same manner, at the same time.

Some creatives absolutely cannot generate a *why* behind their work until they have a strong sense of safety. Some can't channel their frustration, anxiety, and sadness until they can identify what joy feels like first. Some can't connect the dots between their landmarks until they figure out what, exactly, is their own north star.

If you find yourself working through this guidebook and you keep getting stuck in one particular section, or you can't seem to complete the activities in another, take a pause and ask yourself these questions:

- *When I look at this section, how does it make me feel?*

- *Is it possible I'm resistant to this idea because it's hard? Because I'm afraid of the outcome?*

- *Is it possible that I'm actually scared of finishing this project?*

If you do some searching and can clearly say you're not afraid of your own artistic awe or doing the tough, introspective work behind it, then it's time to take a different approach. It's possible that there's some part of your brain that won't let you go forward until you figure something else out. In that case, the solution is to start from your destination.

Here you'll find a separate guidebook for the wild heart that has to work their way up to the big stuff. This is a list of each chapter, starting with *Chapter 12: Find Your Shelter*, and moving backward to *Chapter 6: Pinpoint Your Location*. Beneath each section, you'll find tips for working backwards.

This may be a little messier than you'd like it to be, but that's okay. The point isn't to do it perfectly.

The point is to get out of the forest, no matter which path you take.

GUIDEBOOK IN REVERSE:
AN ALTERNATE ROUTE FOR WILD HEARTS

Find Your Shelter

Take some data on how you best work throughout the day. Complete the tracker activity to take a clear, real-time assessment of how you're working right now. Using what you know about yourself, use the structure diagram to build a day that works for you. Include at least one of the following on each day:

- An activity that feeds your physical, mental, or emotional needs.
- A small step toward reclaiming your creativity, even if that means research, outlining, or free writing.

Listen to the River

Once you have a basic schedule in place to help give you some much-needed stability, pay close attention to which of those soothing activities is giving you joy. Maybe your morning yoga stretches are really vibing with you right now, or those crossword puzzles you do in the bath each night are super relaxing. Once you've figured out where you get the most joy, list your activities on the river rocks in the checkpoint activity.

Signal for Help

So you've started to sort through your emotions and are feeling way clearer. You've maybe even started to dream up a few fresh ideas for a new project. Now's a good time to find yourself a rescue squad. Read the descriptions of the helpers you may need (or already have) on your journey, reach out for support, and run some ideas by them. Sometimes bouncing ideas off of a trusted friend is enough to really ramp up your excitement over a project. A quick note: It's easy to pick up other people's opinions and think they're your own during this process, so make sure you review that structure you made in the beginning, follow your own joy, and stay the course.

Build Your Fire

Now that you know where your joy is coming from, it's time to figure out where it's... well, not. Read this chapter, and use what you've learned about destructive emotions to identify what triggers can lead you astray. And be sure to use the *Stop, Drop, and Roll* activity when everything feels out of control.

Recalculate Your True North

By now, with the help of your closest confidantes, your project should be taking shape into something that could even be doable *and* fun. Here's a good time to do a gut-check with yourself. Have you inadvertently picked up any of your squad members' opinions? Does this project reflect what *you* truly long to make? Make sure to do the Mad Lib activity to double-check that you've heard your own voice.

Uncover Your Landmarks

You've got your squad and you've nailed your voice, but have you figured out all the landmarks you need to uncover to make it happen? Now that you've developed daily habits to keep you healthy, it's time to work through the things that make you, *you*, and inject your art with them. What will make your art a true reflection on you? Work through the landmarks checkpoint to discover your passions, interests, and anything that you're curious about right now. How can you make your work interesting and challenging enough so you'll stick with it for the long haul?

Pinpoint Your Location

Once you have a strong sense of how this will matter to you personally, it's time to go even bigger: How will it matter to the world? Don't settle yourself short here. Don't tell yourself a lie about how your work isn't important. There's no way you can predict the ripples your art will make, so it's best to assume that if it wants to be made through you, it will serve a purpose for someone else. Work through the compass points to find your true direction, what you're really trying to say about the world when all is said and done, and go from there.

You're only getting started, wild heart. Let's go.

SWIM, PADDLE, RUN

The boldest of asking deep questions may require unforeseen flexibility
if we are to accept the answers.
— *Brian Greene*

Let's say that you've been working diligently on your project. You've gone through all the steps and you feel a deeper sense of clarity and connection than you've ever felt before. You've got your rescue squad in place, you've re-discovered your voice, and you're on track with your daily feel-good habits. You even think this might be a little fun.

And then....it happens.

You just don't feel like creating today. You tell your friends it's just a little writer's block flu, that you'll feel better with some Netflix and rest. You'll be back on your feet again in a week.

Only you don't ever feel like getting back up.

The project seems boring now. Or maybe it feels substantially harder: there's a new tension that's creeped up between your shoulder blades as you're hunched over your keyboard. Maybe you've even started to feel more lost than you were when you started.

This is the point in the process where creatives start to doubt themselves and their ideas. But this is the perfect time to rethink your medium, not yourself.

If you've put the intention out there to fill out this entire guidebook with your whole heart, and when you finished you felt good about your project and your map, there's a decent chance this is *it*. This thing you want to make is still important and relevant. The part you may have gotten wrong is exactly *how*.

This has happened to me more times than I can count. What I envisioned as a novel petered out after five thousand words and became a short story, and then morphed into an essay. Poetry expanded into a novel-length work of fiction. My memoir provided the raw material to eventually become this book. In all of those instances, the message I wanted to present to the word stayed on point. The creation itself, however, decided the way I was going about it was all wrong.

There are a lot of reasons we do this to ourselves, but one of the biggest is that we've lost connection with our inner voice—the voice that speaks through our art—along the way. It's super easy to do this, by the way. You tell yourself that you're going to write a screenplay about your chosen topic because you've always written screenplays and you're excellent at it and why wouldn't you write a screenplay?

But your art had other plans from the get-go.

And a lot of times that art won't let you move very far in the wrong direction before it sends you a message—writer's block, spilled paint, tense shoulders, irritability. It slams on the breaks to prevent you from driving yourself straight back into the forest.

So are you ready to listen up?

Are you willing to accept what your inner voice, your creativity is telling you, even if it doesn't immediately make sense?

Below you'll find a listening activity to help your art talk to you. You'll make a character sketch of the project you're currently working on with the same level of detail you would if you were developing a main character in a story. Does your screenplay look like a lumpy old man that smells like Doritos and aftershave? Or is it a spritely girl with a pair of rainbow wings? Either way, make a person out of your piece and be sure to name it. If it helps, you can even draw out a sketch.

Pretend to sit down with your piece in front of you and ask it some or all of these interview questions:

- *What do you think the most important part of your work is?*
- *What's the least important part?*
- *What's your favorite thing to do for fun?*
- *What makes you absolutely miserable?*
- *If you had one message to give to the world, what would it be?*
- *How would you most like the world to see you?*

Take note of what you write down. Often times your own subconscious will surprise you with the answers.

One of the ways I finally figured out that my memoir was never meant to be a memoir was by having a very similar chat with it. In my interview, my memoir became my mother, and she gently reminded me that she didn't want her existence defined by the end of her life—she had been more than illness and chaos. She also reminded me that the essence of her was a creator, someone who liked to bring joy to others by making things.

That stuck with me.

I was more than disappointed that all of those hours and sweat that had gone into that memoir seemed pointless. It's been years since I wrote it, but the lessons I took from that process were invaluable. I got to know myself and my family's struggle with creativity intimately. I distilled my own feelings and message around what it meant to be a creative being in the world, and that story developed into a compass point to guide creatives, no matter what, for the rest of my life.

It resulted in this big, beautiful book of my heart.

I'd say it wasn't all that pointless.

It wasn't that bad after all.

ALLOWING THE FLOW

Maybe the journey isn't so much about becoming anything.
Maybe it's about un-becoming everything that isn't really you,
so you can be who you were meant to be in the first place.
— *Paulo Coelho*

Imagine a river full of rocks.

You can tell that it used to flow freely, but something must have happened to it. Maybe the rocks fell from the side of a cliff. Maybe they rolled down a hill. Maybe someone or something put them here, but anyway, it doesn't matter how they got here. What matters is that they're clogging up the natural flow of the water.

Imagine the story of *you*.

Think of every memory, emotion, relationship, cultural and personal belief that has woven itself into your DNA to make you who you are. How many of those pieces of your past are wounds that weight you down instead of rafts you can ride down the river?

So many creatives struggle with how to get the work done, how to make the time, how to be "productive." We obsess over stickers on a calendar, daily word counts, social competition and internal pressure. We endlessly tinker with time management, when really we need to be talking about energy management.

Back to the river. Imagine that river is your creative flow, and every physical, emotional, mental, and spiritual wound you've ever suffered through is a rock. Each rock—no matter if it's a boulder or a pebble—deters the river's natural flow toward joyful creativity. Each rock holds us back from recognizing that brilliant, off-the-wall idea that you don't yet realize you'd love to write. Each rock hinders you from fully expressing yourself to your highest potential, and no matter how much we plan and outline and escape, we'll continue to get in our own way until we remove the rocks.

When we remove the rocks—or at least most of them—the river flows freely. Time expands, events and people fall into place, and we find ourselves naturally drawn to projects that are a joy to work on, even when they challenge us. It's happiness with our work and lives, not time management tips, that's the key to productivity. You can do so much more when your art is aligned with who you are when you allow the flow.

Keep this in mind when you're feeling stuck on a project. Remember if you're using this project as a tool to help you excavate the wound, it will be hard work. You're going to sweat. You'll be sore, and sometimes sad, and everything will hurt. But *when* you get through this, you will have removed a big-ass boulder, and your life and art will be so much better off for it.

Don't be afraid to go back through the parts of this book that will help you heal those stubborn wounds. Don't be afraid to seek whatever help you need to uncover who you are after the pain has been removed. Don't be afraid to seek wholenesss, and support, and love.

Remind yourself that you're going to push through the hard stuff so you can stop giving away your creativity to institutions and toxic relationships. That you're doing this so you can stop patching up holes in a sinking raft instead of building a new one from the best parts of *you*.

Allow the flow.

And ride the river home.

BE OKAY WITH
GETTING LOST

Not all those who wander are lost — J. R. R. Tolkien

There's one last thing I haven't told you yet, but it's probably the most important thing of all.

In the end, you have to learn to be okay with getting lost.

Making something out of nothing is not a linear process and it never will be. We can't control the way our synapses fire when they think up an idea and which pieces of our environment will make a bridge between connections that day, or if we'll miss it all together. The best we can do is learn ourselves deeply, build a life around who we are, what we need, and our intention to do this work in the world. That part is ours to harness. The rest of it—the true essence of creativity—is beyond our knowing and control.

We have to understand that if we are explorers of what it means to be human, we will lose ourselves on our expeditions, again and again. The getting lost part is inevitable. We will encounter seasons that are more difficult to bear than others and it will feel damn near impossible to open up that sketchbook or pick up that guitar again. But you have to. You must. The world needs your art now more than ever. This is your sacred assignment.

There's no reason to fear the forest anymore.

Now you have the tools, wild heart, to find your way out once again.

I can't wait to see what you create.

PART FOUR

ADDITIONAL CHECKPOINTS
& RESOURCES

M.A.S.H.
Idea Generator

1. Choose a number between 5 - 16.
2. Fill out this sheet with various elements.
3. Start at the top left box and move clockwise, counting to the number you chose. When you reach that line, cross it off. Keep going until you have only ONE item in each box. Use these four things for a new idea!

MEANING (THEME)
Ex: identity, loss, etc.

1._____

2. _____

3. _____

4. _____

ADD-INS (EXTRAS)
Ex: flamethrower, unicorn, wand

5._____

6. _____

7. _____

8. _____

SURPRISE (TWIST)
Ex: plane crash, betrayal, etc.

13._____

14. _____

15. _____

16. _____

HERO (MAIN CHARACTER)

9._____

10. _____

11. _____

12. _____

Productivity Tracker

Use this tool in conjunction with the energy trackers at the end of Chapter 12. Once you've gone through your new, revamped schedule for a week, calculate how many hours you've spent resting, playing, creating, working, and managing tasks. Try to get all five parts of the circle as even as possible. Fill in each pie piece with activities that apply for each.

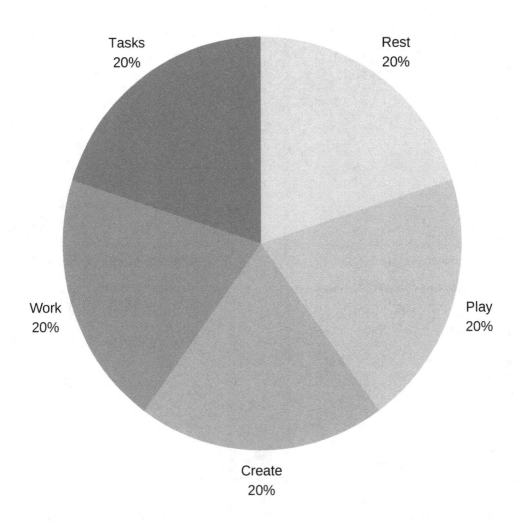

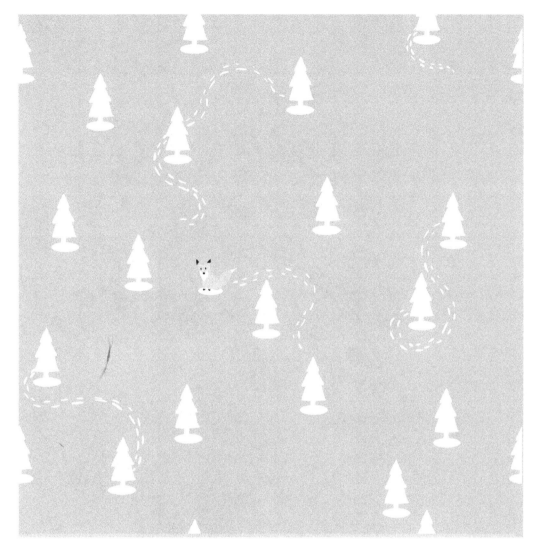

Map Your Progress

Set a small goal for your project. Each time you finish a chapter, song, painting, or anything else color in a tree above.

Goal: _____

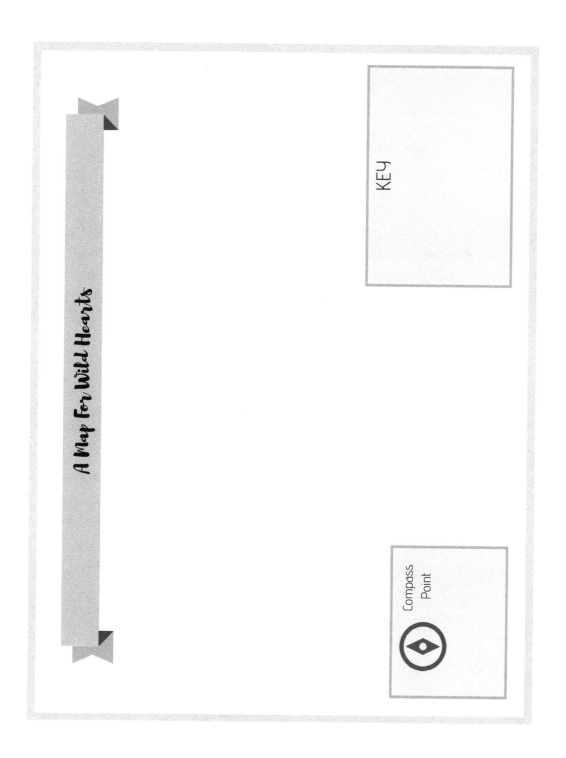

A Map For Wild Hearts

KEY

Compass
Point

ACKNOWLEDGEMENTS

No one creates in a vacuum, and I was lucky enough to make this book with guidance and distraction from the purest artists I know: Sam and Violet Hannah. Their little voices reminded me not to take myself to seriously, their fingerprints on my computer keys let me know I can always undo what someone else put in place for me when I wasn't looking. I'll cherish the time we all sat at the dining room table, each in our own headspace, creating beautiful things together.

To Matt, my husband, is pretty much the best sort of partner any creative can ask for: generous with his time and energy, willing to take on the extra load, and absolutely unwilling to put up with my bullshit. Thank you. I needed that.

To the Wild Hearts OGs—Becca, Aimée, Kelsey, Zack, Kristin—you guys are so special to me. I'll cherish our time at the lake house together for the rest of my life. You make me better as a writer and a human being.

To the dream team that made all the pieces of this book fit together seamlessly—Patricia, Molly, Keri—you made this book into the best version of itself. And Austin, you get your own shoutout for the cover because it's dope as hell and your design skills are top notch. I can't thank you all enough.

And to the original Wild Heart OGs—my mom and grandma. If I have one ounce of the creativity, intuition, and kindness you had, I'll be all right.

ABOUT THE AUTHOR

Andrea Hannah is an award-winning author, essayist, and workshop leader. Her work has appeared in Bustle, HuffPost, Harness Magazine, and more. She teaches on living a healthy creative life at her Wild Heart retreats and writes about making art on Twitter and Instagram (**@andeehannah**).

You can also find her at:

WWW.ANDREAHANNAH.COM

CPSIA information can be obtained
at www.ICGtesting.com
Printed in the USA
BVHW012122120819
555749BV00007B/121/P

9 780578 521725